The Collected Poems of

Israel Aszendorf

Second Edition

Translated and Edited by Alexander Ashendorf

ISBN – 978-1793078780

Library of Congress Control Number: 2019900039
Alexander Ashendorf, Staten Island, NY

Kindle Direct Publishing

Contact: alexashendorf@gmail.com

To
   The memory of my father
   Israel Aszendorf.

Table of Contents

Poems Featured in Both *Monday Morning* and *Woe and Wander*

Poems Featured in both *Greetings From Far*, and *Woe and Wander*

From **Woe and Wander** (1950)

From **Last Writings** (1958)

Additional Poems

From the **Miniatures**

The Life and Works of Israel Aszendorf, 1909-1956

Born in Mielnitsa in Polish Galitsia, grew up in Lemberg/Lvov (Now Lviv, in the Ukraine). Studied in Hebrew school and later in a teachers' seminary. Started writing in his youth. Debuted with a poem in 1927, in *Unzer Hofenung* and in *Yungt-veker* (Youth alarm), *Folkstzeitung* (People's Newspaper) and *Literarishe Bleter* (Literary Leaves) in Warsaw and Lemberg.

Israel Aszendorf (on left) with family in Poland before WW2

Was secretary of YIVO and the Jewish theater league in Lemberg. In the 1930's he was, along with Rachel Korn, S. Imber, Ber Horowitz and others, part of the contribution (*Tsushteyer)* group. Adapted two works of A. Goldfaden for the theater: '*Bar Kokhba*', and '*Di Broder Zinger*' (The Brother singers) which played in Warsaw in 1938 and 39.

Israel Aszendorf (fifth from left) and my mother Rachel (eighth from left) next to Abraham Zack, Yitzhak Yanasovitch, Moyshe Knapheis, and other fellow authors in Paris, early 50'.

From 1939 to 1945, he lived in the Soviet Union, mostly in Tashkent, (in today's Uzbekistan.) worked as a medic and some other odd jobs, and was a friend of the poet Naum Bomzeh. In 1945 he returned to Poland where he found that his entire immediate family of five brothers a sister and mother, had perished in the Holocaust. Was active in reconstruction attempts of Jewish life in Poland after the war. Aided with the Jewish theater in Lodz and wrote children's poems. In 1948 he went to Paris, where he married and had a son. Was a contributing editor of the literary journal *'Kiyum'* (Existence). In 1951, he received the Alexander Shapiro award for creativity for his '*King Saul*' which he shared with H. Leyvick. In 1952 he received the *Yud Lamed-Peretz* prize from the '*Kultur Kongres*' for the same work. In the early fifties he visited Israel, and at one point was in negotiations with the national theater '*Habima*' for featuring his play *King Saul* which had been translated to Hebrew. however, the Israeli cultural and theater establishment of the day did not look favorably on Yiddish as it was anathema to a new nation struggling to unite and renew itself in Hebrew, and he felt that he was getting the cold shoulder. In 1953 he immigrated to Argentina where he worked as a teacher of Hebrew language, and Yiddish literature in a teachers' seminary, a collaborator in the '*Yiddishe Tseitung*', and as an inspector of Jewish schools.

Rachel and Israel Aszendorf (mom & dad). Paris, circa. 1951

He was vice president of the Jewish writers' union in Buenos Aires. Published in *Tsukunft* (Future), and *Yiddisher Kempfer* (Jewish fighter), in New York and *'Goldene Keit'* in Tel-Aviv. Several of his poems had been translated to Hebrew by Shimshon Meltzer, and one story of his: 'A relative', by Rachel Auerbach. Another story 'The strange story of Haim Haykel the cat' and the poem 'Dust' were translated to Spanish and appeared in print in Argentina. His articles, poems and stories have appeared in a multitude of Yiddish newspapers in Europe, Israel, and throughout south America, Canada, South Africa and the U.S.

Speaking at an award ceremony (probably) in Buenos Aires

Historical Background

Secular Yiddish literature came into bloom in the late nineteenth century Russia, with the works of Shalom Aleichem, Mendele

Moykher Sforym and Y.L. Peretz, who in their stories described the transition of the Jewish people in Eastern Europe from poverty religiosity and tradition, to immigration to better places and secularism, all influenced by the movements of the Jewish Enlightenment, Zionism, and by the pogroms.

This literary movement was significant, until some years after the second world war.

With the destruction of a large population of Yiddish speakers in the Holocaust, the survivors dying out, and most of the following generations abandoning Yiddish as their Jewish vernacular, the amount and quality of Yiddish literature written since, has shrunk tremendously.

In his poems, stories and plays, Israel Aszendorf traces Jewish life in the early twentieth century shtetl, all the way through the prewar socialist revolutionary zeal, WWII, the life of a displaced Jew in Europe, and then his attempts to build a new life away from Europe, in Argentina. Many stories are autobiographical at least to some degree, and as such, one could consider the total body of work as describing a history of 'secular' Jewish life between the mid-twenties and early fifties of the twentieth century.

A task he did not accomplish was the writing and publication of *'King Solomon'*, his third book in the trilogy of the first three Israelite kings, and also the publication of other plays, a children's story book, and other short stories, which I (his son Alexander) have gathered, translated and am bringing to print in this and sister volumes. Some of his work had been commented on and showcased mostly in the 1950's in the following publications:

Yiddishe Shriften, (Lodz). *Unzer vart* (Paris). *Yiddishe Tseitung* (Buenos Aires) *Literarishe Bleter, and Kiyum* (Paris), *Argentiner Beymlech* and *Di Prese* (Buenos Aires). *Unzer Shtimeh (Paris), Lashon un Leben* (London) *Yiddishe Kultur* (New York) *Goldene Keyt,* (Tel Aviv). *Der Morgen Journal, Der Shpigel* (Buenos Aires) *Keneder Odler* (Canada) *Unzer Gedank, La Vie Juive* (Paris) *Afrikaner Yiddishe Tseitung* (South Africa), *Comentario,* (Buenos Aires) and *Havaner Leben* in Cuba.

His work had been commented on by the following colleagues and critics: Melekh Ravitch (My Lexicon). The Yiddish Lexicon, Moyshe Knapheiss, Y. Harn, R. Feder, Gabriel Weismann, Isaac Yanasovitch, Melech Tchemney, Mates Dytch, Abraham Zack, Dr. A. Mukdony, Dr. Shlomo Bikel, Y. Freilied, Yaakov Glantz, Yaakov Glatshtein, Abraham Shulman, Haim Leib Fooks, Rachel Auerbach, A. Domankevitch, and Yaakov Botoshanski.

His main publications:

In a Great Unknown City, **Poem**	1932	In a Groyseh Fremdeh Shtot
Monday Morning, **Poems**	1937	Montik Inderfri
Greetings From Far, **Poems**	1939	Grissen in der Veit
Premonition and Reality **Poems**	1941	Anung un Var (lost)
King Saul **, Play**	1948	Der Meylekh Shaul
Woe and Wander, **Poems**	1950	Vey un Vander
Partners in Fate, **Stories**	1953	Shutafim fun Goyral
King David, **Play**	1956	Der Meylekh David
Last Writings, **Poems, stories & plays** (Posthumously)	1958	Letsteh Shriften

The last five books on the list above, can be read in Yiddish on the internet archive (Open Library.org) or the national Yiddish book center/ Spielberg Digital Library. The top first three, as well as some other plays, poems and stories, which are not available on line, I plan to send to them in the near future.

The first three publications, *In a Great Unknown City, Monday Morning* and *Greetings From Far*, contain poems written between the first and second world wars. They are the works of a poet deeply moved, not only by the economic plight of his immediate family, but also, of humanity at large: the factory worker and the common man. It was a time of revolutionary zeal, when in the depressed and war-ravaged Europe of the time, socialism and unionism had more of an appeal than they have today. Also, to be young and idealistic also meant, in many cases to be a socialist.

(My mother once told me that when he worked for his brother's business, he organized the workers and they declared a strike). His next book of poems, *Woe and Wander* (1950) seems like more of a mature work and has more of an expanded subject matter. It contains poems from different periods: i.e. early childhood and the Holocaust, and some with a more of an abstract and/or lyrical tone, such as *Beards*, *Letters* and *Dust*. The book also has some of his earlier poems reworked and presented there.

King Saul and *King David*, are two plays about the first two kings of Israel, written as 'biblical poems'. As mentioned above, the intended third and final one in the trilogy was never written.

Partners in fate, contains 10 Stories. It introduces Israel Aszendorf's alter ego, David Farber. An exception in this book is *The Strange Story of Haim Haykel the Cat,* which unlike all other stories in this book, is of pure fantasy.

Last writings, is a posthumous compendium of stories, poems, one acts, and miniatures.

In his introduction to *Vey un Vander* (Woe and wander) he mentions that some works were lost during the war: the poem *Uriel*

Acosta, I Invite you to a Masquerade Ball, and the book *Anung* un *Var* (Premonition/news, and reality) as well as many others. *I Invite you to a Masquerade Ball,* had been found, but not so other ones. Obviously, I will be grateful to hear from anyone with possession or knowledge of lost work. At the time of his death he was about to publish a book with ten one act plays, a children's storybook, and as noted above had plans for writing *'King Solomon'*, the third book in the trilogy of the kings. Additionally, his plan-book shows many ideas for additional short stories. Material which had been published in newspapers at the time, or remained unpublished in a book form, and some material from the family archive is being brought to print in this series.

Translator's Note

It is more than sixty years since my father's untimely death in Argentina, and I am older now than my father was when he died.

Until very recently, I didn't know any Yiddish and could not read any of his work. After my father's death my mother who was born in Aden and didn't speak Yiddish, moved us to Israel; Israel had adopted a newly refurbished Hebrew as its national language as both a practical and political necessity. Yiddish, being a Germanic language, foreign in sound and bearing different cultural connotations, the Jewish immigrants coming from Arab countries would not speak it. Also, Yiddish met with the disfavor of the young country's leaders who associated it with an old image of an oppressed diaspora Jew, and its study was suppressed. As for myself, I'd left Israel in the mid 80's and came to the U.S. to start a new life. I had to concentrate on English and so I took up the study of Yiddish, late in life.

Of the total body of work, I know of very few pieces which had been translated into Hebrew, English and Spanish, and just like the works of many other Yiddish writers, his works too, have remained until now, mostly untouched. Since the end of WWII, secular Yiddish literature has suffered a reduction in the number of both readers and literary works. By my reckoning Yiddish users today are of three types: The Ultra-Orthodox community, who is not the main customer of modern secular Yiddish writing. Old secular Jews who still remain since the 'old days' of the middle of the 20th century, and the young generation where Yiddish has met with renewed interest. However, the resurgence of Yiddish among some young people is not the same as having entire communities of Jews using it as their vernacular, and so, with the destruction of European Jewry, their mass migration to the United States and Israel, and increased political freedom and prosperity, came more assimilation and

My father and I on vacation. Argentina, 1955

abandonment of their roots. Some Jews consider this process a second holocaust, a cultural one...

These trends didn't bode well for my father's work being sought in its original form. With the continuation of the current trend and dwindling in the number of potential readers, chances are that my father's work would disappear, so I decided to undertake its translation.

In the process of editing the material I was faced with the dilemma of **What not to publish**. Consequently, while publishing everything, makes the collection 'definitive', the quality of the collection, especially as pertains to some poems and miniatures, is not, shall we say, consistent. I decided, however, that since these three books are not only 'In memory of...' but also 'The collected works of...' I would include everything I had.

Eighteen of the poems in *Woe and Wander* had previously appeared in *Monday Morning* and *Greetings from Far*. one poem: *A Jewish Woman* was featured in *Last Writings* and was named *Spring*. When translating these poems, I initially thought of favoring the writer's preference, ostensibly, his later version, however, I soon realized that once translated, the small differences between the versions, became less significant, and so, I decided to merge the small differences into one version.

THIS IS A SECOND, REVISED EDITION

Due to a technical mishap, the Feb. 16, 2018 first printing of the 3 books in this series, was based on a 'proof', unedited version, and had to be withdrawn from the market.

Please use the books at hand (marked '*Second Edition*' on the cover and title page) as replacement, and destroy the old version.

New-York, January, 2019.

In a Great Unknown City: A note on the translation.

This poem came out all by itself in one book in 1932. It is the longest of his poems, and compared to many of the following poems, it is not only a 'socially conscious' one, but also, one steeped in socialistic fervor and compassion for the common man, or dare I say... proletariat. It was written between the 1st and 2nd world wars when the young impressionable author was encountering economic depression in the big city of Lemberg (now Lviv), and socialism was all the rage. The reader is advised to proceed with caution; this poem is different from all the rest in its length and abstractions, and should not set the reader's expectations for what is yet to come. I would even recommend, skipping it altogether and approaching it later.

In a Great Unknown City (1932)

A man comes to a great unknown city,
He arrives with curiosity and expectations
With enthusiasm and delight.
But soon he is disappointed and embittered,
Hear him tell his story.

I, to a great unknown city did come.
I'd heard of wondrous inventions, great scope,
Which in iron and wood, men had wrought
Philosophers pondered and poets sang.
To see the works and the pride of
Past generations – I came. And some
Came to obtain, what by brothers and sisters
Was built, with tears, sweat and blood.
Spellbound I go through the city streets;
It's a wondrous world, riches flow
To me from all sides, so much so
That I, the man, want to kneel down and ask:
Why are there so few memorials in town.

I, to a great unknown city did come:
I looked for people, I looked for bread,
And found people bound under seven locks.
And under locks seven — I also found bread,
Over which, wealth raised its drunken head
And a mouth in need, clogged up with a fist.
Wretchedness cries from cellar to roof
The hungry man breaks through mountains of peril,
But to break into food stores, he is too weak!

I, to a great unknown city did come.
And there I came, furious, forlorn,
My dream crucified on all doors,
Proceeding to every threshold.
Skyscrapers, showcases, billboards mock me.
Who needs you here?
In my blindness I thought I was quite exalted
And saw: I was rather slavish, a fool:
Quite a clown!
My books had made me so alien, so void
Till I left them behind in the trash.
I saw up-ahead a great curious life
I've taken to reading it all.

He drags himself around, across
The big unknown city. Sees drunkenness
And crime. Twists himself between walls
Dreams of bread and a bed,
But the bread in the dream is not filling
And the bed isn't warm.

It is night.
Slowly cease the glittering charms.
Homeless I pace, cross the big foreign town.
A light in a lantern burns dim.
From the heavens are smiling cold stars.
The lavish streets doze, the heads in the tousled hair
Of the black gypsy whore – the night.

A man stands by a gate, it is dark and closed.
Ringing and ringing, who knows
If his child is ill, and he's calling for help?
Or perhaps has a knife, concealed in his coat
Now smelling the blood; and tomorrow, at last…

From coffee houses the drunk turn home, singing.
From whore-houses, men go home, saunter, sedate.

From the tavern breaks an obscure passing light,
Hoarse clangs. From there, a pair of louts
With a street girl went out; one sings a song
She's singing too. The other one whistles along:
Pij! pij! pij! Fweet, pij!

It is night.
I ramble on through the streets; a gust of wind makes me shiver
Something grabs me inside, crying, lamenting so deep.
Ah, what should I do? I've been desolate, lonesome, alone,
On which threshold is my sick head lying, on which stone?
I stray through the streets, and hear, hotels calling and crying:
I have twenty beds!
I have fifty beds!
I have a hundred vacant beds!
Beds of finest wood, pillows of down
Warm and light, rugs under your feet,
Men-servants, and women-servants
At your door.

I am tired; I cling to a cold wall.
Here I will probably lie, till dawn.
But soon, there's a light in a window across,

Someone beckons: come, come up my love!
I go up; the table is loaded with liquor and food.
I eat, I drink, and cannot, no cannot be content.
I toss in bed; covered with thick fine spreads,
But that doesn't work. A terror awakens inside,
Ah, will I ever be sated? Keep warm?
I wake up and find: all my body parts intact.
The day is graying; streetcars ring.
Blooming are threshold and stair,
And a street sweeper sweeps my night
Of dogged despair.

He looks for work – finds none.
Neither can he feel joy from creating
Or commanding creation. He cries,
Blasphemes and carries on.

Too often I've turned to people for work,
But the empty-handed, they would not help
Daily I've looked for work in the papers, but papers
Parade the pent-up cries of thousands like me
In each town, in each place.
It is food for want, suicide and despair.
And I have found more: someone is looking to buy
A villa. In a village near the mountains, with windows to
River and woods, but no one looked for, nor wanted a thing
From hands that are willing, to carry some brick,
Carry burdens, cut stones.

I have gone 'cross the city, met men by a building
Very joyously growing. Every inch it goes up
Through me anger mounts, and I have figured thus:
Unknown to me is the joy of building, and still unknown is
The joy of a place to rest my body and gray tired head.

I have walked 'cross the city and saw a wood-shop
Happily joining parts of trees and lives,
But I remained still. Recalling days and years:
Unknown to me is the joy of a hammer and saw, and unknown
Still, the joy of a bed and table in a private abode.

I have walked 'cross the city; in the street saw a bake-shop
The oven like a mouth with a red joyous laugh.
Something had, painfully twitched my face, pallid and slim.
Ah, unknown to me is the joy of baking and still unknown,
Is the joy of fresh cake and bread — puffy and white.

I have walked 'cross the city and it was springing free
With some of its pain, I frightfully shouted, was wild
All inside, but did not make a sound, I became myself
A great cry: against all of the trampling, all the past ages,
And against all, that to them is attached.
In a vintage stained shirt, Bergson, Tagore, in my head,
I've been filled with memories, and hunger for black bread!

Truly, my hands are now, not such that possess or create.
My hands are two loaded weapons that don't wait for mercy
And don't wait for grace.

The speech of an unemployed man, in the midst of a big
unknown city.

And it is a pregnant time,
Twins in her belly:
Fall and rise.

It is indeed quiet, why does it seem,
That I walk in a city besieged?
In every eye, such dumb fear.
All boroughs are seized by hunger, and calm,
Ignored and unseen die the old,
Die the young.
Sick wives are descending on restaurant trash
Maybe from there they will bring something home.
Your twelve year old life does not ask for a thing
Except a warm bed for the night.

Through firemen, someone runs out of a house:
Are there really, no more people inside?

I see a world shrieking in clutches of want
Over it hangs, not green, but red spring.
There, I see life; there, I also see death;
Life and death I see there like twins.
Everywhere: being lost, everywhere: disarray,
Hindrance, turmoil. In the people I feel
A growth, a fermenting, a rising,
What once took years, now is done in a day.
Wretchedness binds the lost stones of the road.
They melt; they lock together in one strong wall.
A word that is pure out of sorrow. bright out of joy
A word so equally wondrous, mundane:
Comrade! A master-key, to rule all the rest.
A word that breaks walls between peoples and creeds.
Unites and bonds them into one single class
A bright message shining, over all heads:
The florid phrase: 'morning' – a new lovely day!

A music band playing, now, ask all the people:
Isn't everyone here celebrating this triumph?

A meeting. A voice like an ax in the midst of the thicket of
voices:
This world is a great terminus – some await the hereafter
Waiting and waiting; but the old, the whores, and the traitors,
We are not those who wait, we are those who are coming!

A man had strayed and strayed
Until he found out that the grave
Of which he was terrified, was a wellspring.

What would I do now if it weren't for you?
A man broken of terror and want, in the midst
Of a world that tastes like old age and sloth?
In each form seeing specters, in every light — clouds
Every tree burning, all windows closed.
Or lie down in a bar with drunks and whores
Rebellious, with thieves louts and rogues.

There are women, I've heard it said, that
Pull you out with uncanny strength.
Each organ of yours is a key, under their touch.
The gray week now colorful, a holiday fest.
Their lives are a lilting spellbound waltz,
Their body's your dream-land, all else you forget.
There is one I recall, she worked at a plant,
When I used to touch her, her gaze seemed to me
So tired and sad, that soon I was, ashamed to touch.
A second one dreaded I should stay too long,
What do you do, how to handle rebuffs?
A third, brought me her heart like a wound to be healed
But what could I say, about *my* heart?

No way out. I know clearly, for sure:
Two bloods in my veins – my own, and the truth.
Not numbing the pain, not falling asleep, inciting the mind
The bandages off; let blood leak out of all wounds —
No way out. Through solitude, hardship and want.
Through nights of inner struggle, days of external war
A voice tearing through:
All can now hear it inside:
—Something wondrous, something great is about to be born!
Comrades, you heard? Heard a lost cry?
Ah, you should know: it is from a man in great sorrow.
One who has without mercy, cut with his teeth

His own umbilical cord.
A man that strayed and strayed till he found
That the pit he was scared of, was a bountiful spring.

Behold: he is rinsing the dust, he sinks in, and draws
Bucketfulls of faith, bucketfulls of calm.

A little stream flows into the sea
And behold:
Soon comes a storm.

It was a sunny, gentle start.
One by one opened: workroom, business and shop.
From bakeries, carts began to bring to the stores:
Bread, pastries, puffed rolls.
In the butcher-shops, they hung
Juicy chunks of meat, of cattle and calf
With a new day the city, is now waking up!
As if never before it had smelled such wealth.
Provoked with richness, rising at dawn,
Like a young lovely woman, that's all made up
And prevented from leaving the house.
A quiet day, but somehow it seemed,
That it was the silence of people in fear.
The enemy must not, hear a rustle, and find it.
A silence, as if engulfing the sick, not waking them up.
Like, before a storm, or saying hello.

And lo: one by one, from street corners they come,
One, a second, a third. And presently striding, pacing
The clock-work of loneliness, hunger.
Mutiny in the eye and a cramp in the finger
Like a cloud tearing from the gray piece of want,
In the middle of rich streets falls down and flows.
One starts with a song another one joins, and soon,
A song shoots up like a fine machined part!
And suddenly – gallops a horse, shiny guns cracking.
A cry – a fall. A cry – a fall. A cry – a fall!
A child tipped over, was trampled and buried
Jesus will jump from the cross and of horror freeze up.
Blood is boiling, faces flush in the danger
Through the air shrieking stones pulling out of the pavement
And the powers untrammeled, like steam in a kettle –
Burst out; they tear out in a bloody combat.

Some rich mister was caught in the middle, pulled in.
But soon escaped into a nearby commode
Well, the fury subsided, thank God!
Put up in a café, one more glass of strong wine.
A peasant woman had in a rush, spilled some milk
And the milk got mixed with the blood.
And carts travel far with screaming ads.

Charlie Chaplin! Harold Lloyd! Fervor and smack!
Oodles of laughter! Laugh till you cry, Laugh till you die!

Through a wound he was healed
From under the bridge, his voice
Is heard: upwards it moves,
Upwards it is going on with flesh
Flowing with blood, it is done!

From heaven drips cold rain, from the wound – warm blood
I don't remember when I received that cut,
The deep cut in my body from a sharp sword.
I remember but a cry from some people, a neigh from a horse.
I remember: standing in the first row, and a call
Issued forth like a hot piece of lead.
And then, chaos; and then – to where the gaze leads.
Till I saw it here under the bridge.

From heaven drips cold rain, from the wound – warm blood
Hunger exploded a summer day like dynamite.
But again in homes sit the lonely and listen to none,
How loneliness calls from each bend: what will it be?
How many more times, how many more times
Can we disperse?
In hospital beds the wounded may cry
In dungeons in silence united they lie, and understand
That the new tablets are, engraved with teeth not with hands.

From heaven drips cold rain, from the wound – warm blood.
Who's sneaking in here? Who silently steps in the dark?
Who's by the wall shuffling by?
Stranger, don't fear; I extend to you a friendly hand.
Are you a wanderer? Holy is, each step and each stride.
Why travel far, when justice is already at hand
You're a thief? Why steal a spoon in fear, when you
Can conquer a world with struggle and joy.

From heaven drips cold rain, from the wound – warm blood.
Friend! Rip my shirt and bandage my wound!
Marvel on how I don't wail, groan or whine.
Marvel on how I bite off that shout with my teeth
Know, that the rage is not for being lost, but for being reborn
Not with mother's cry and blood, but with your own.

From heaven drips cold rain, from the wound – warm blood!
But not from despair, friend, it will be good, it will be good.
We have been bearing the pain in solitude.
Let's now bear it with the multitudes.
Behold: an old drunken peasant-woman vomiting,
All gets absorbed in a ditch.
This is the old world; she totters to an everlasting sleep.
A world reborn, blooming with whores out of mildew and moss,
From earth into heaven rises a star, that casts a dark shadow on all.

Monday Morning (1937)

Monday Morning

Who burped out the Sabbath and who vomited out Sunday?
You get up, get dressed and prepare for the weekdays. It is
Monday morning.

There will be a week of worry and toil. So much which hasn't
been accomplished awaits. It either must be corrected or
dismantled. But don't worry yourself. You are armed. You have
within, your possessions:

A hammer, a drill and a saw. So you will cut through, bore
through; break a path through the six days.

In your window and in Monday's, it is now grey. Only in
Monday's, the head of an old man peers in. In yours – the
youthful day. Monday is not only the first day of the week,
it knows; It can be the first day in Genesis.

Family

Eviction

Once we owned a house in the shtetl
But mother had constantly dreamt of a day
When she'd switch that house for another;
With a garden with greens, and with flowers.
If she wanted peas or beans for the soup
She could go and pick them herself.
If she wanted an onion or carrot for stew
In the garden she could find that too,
From the best and the finest, not a thing to be bought.
Under the window — it would all grow.

But since father lay sick for quite a long time
And the debts were increasing
The house had to be sold
And all roads lead to town.
Here is a doctor for father, and a hospital;
Here, for the young brothers – a school.
And here you can be a customer
For a loaf of bread or a cellar abode.

The moment she saw the new place,
She crossed her arms in protest:
She must whitewash the owner's walls?
Not in his life!
And scrub the owner's floor?
She hasn't yet lost her mind!
She should polish the owner's windows?
No! She will live here the way it is!
And she spent a long time in the dwelling.
Like in a foreign hotel.
But soon, there began to appear

Demands from the landlord for rent
For three months for six, for a year.
So to her it was clear:
A great peril is creeping in here,
And each corner became more beloved
She was ever reminded of the past.
One early morning, on the window sill
There, even grew a plant.

Each time mother went to the landlord
She would don her velvet dress.
She would put on, her black widow's veil,
(It might possibly touch his heart)
Polished her tattered shoes –
And go to the landlord against the eviction
To plead.

And when she is home in the evening,
Her eyes are puffy from tears,
We go to sleep, and she paces at length
Looks at the table, the mirror, the beds.
All in here is essential, is needed.
Where will she now put her things — in the street?
And over the sleeping children she peeks,
Where will they sleep now, under which bridge?
On the wall she sees her own shadow,
Hunched over and shaking, and just to herself
She remembers and thinks: oh,
What I have lived to see, in my old years!

Early morning – it is still dark.
Twisted up in a corner, mother lies on the bed.
On her face every wrinkle imprinted with dread.
She lies in her dress, with her shoes, frozen, stiff.
As if she already, lies in the street.
And over her come – autumn wind and rain.

My Brother Writes From the Shtetl

The shelves get vacant by the hour
There's almost nothing in the drawers
Everybody borrows, but I pay with cash.
The best hopes from my younger days,
Now will never come to pass.

And the child, I don't know what he wants.
He cries and cries and cries: it makes me think,
That what mutely cries in me,
Is being voiced by him.

I read the letter and I know:
I must reply with hopeful words,
And we cannot abandon hope.
A younger person – after all would last…

Only I don't do it, I cannot!
I know: for him there is no hope.
He will die – die – die.
He, and his whole shopkeeper tribe.

Who do you chastise – your own brother?
When we were small didn't we lie in the same bed?

I also lay with someone else in the same bed.
He was a peasant from the Vohlin region.
And it was not at home – it was in prison.
We lay close and talked, all through the night.
Not only were our bodies near but also something more,
Like at the time when we were young.

Did we not go to the same school?

I've now forgotten that which I once learned,
And that which I am learning now – to you is strange.
I'm not what I once was, you would not recognize me
I know already what are factory, war and prison.
And I am distant from your tribe.

And the voice of blood? The voice demands and calls!

Want and loneliness had sucked that blood away –
Of that blood no trace remains.
Why even mention what is clear to all:
It's not important where the blood came from
But why it's spilled and where it goes.

And your child? For now, he is still creeping on all fours
When he can walk, he'll walk away.
He cries? He will grow older, grasp the danger
His tears will cease and he will yell! Demand!

… Now it's evening. I see you in your shop
Standing at the threshold, bent-over and hushed,
You wait. What are you waiting for my brother?
You say: for a better time? A sunny day?
Only the saintly tailor got assurances*
Cross over the threshold, to the street
On the shop sign you will see…
Why are you trembling and so pale?
I see there just one word and it is: death!

---

* A reference to a tailor who in the city of Prague, volunteered to take the blame
for the death of a king, and thus save a whole Jewish community from death.
He was tortured, executed, and became known as the 'Holy Tailor'

Around me

A Patcher* Such as This

A patcher such as this
With a head like a thimble, a neck – like a finger
With a belt on his belly, which is always loose.
With bloodless veins, like broken threads, frail,
Which cannot understand, what kind of force
Keeps him alive, and rejuvenates ...

A patcher such as this
Who just about survives on cold potatoes
And some kasha which is really good and festive.
And next, a borscht, a red one, hot like fire.
But wine – what's that? It only mixes up your head.
And anyway it is too dear.

A patcher such as this
In these numbered days of rest and peace.
With a sweet glass of mead and a hopeful song
All the corners in the house sparkle and shine.
So whose world is it, whose is it now
If not his own? ...

---

* Derogatory: a low skill tailor

The Scandal Begins

The scandal started in March:
Love-stricken cats began to meow in verse,
And the meowing was heard from attics in homes.
In the library there was a sudden lack, of books on love –
So, wealthy widows went to the seamstress demanding
That their clothes be made dainty and long,
And sixteen year olds, began to wake up
Sweating in the middle of the night. They tossed off
Their blankets and covers,
Even old ugly maids turned bold
Their look – misleading, and full of the evil urge.

And the master of the insolent factory felt it as well,
Even though he was forty years old,
And had children four.
He invited the seventeen year old worker girl to a hotel.
Promised her a silky, summery dress, but she
(Who was a person who could awaken nature and lust)
Did not show up, and was fired from her job at the plant.

Once There was a Home

Once there was a home.
(Oh, just listen to this!)
And home, simply means:
A roof over your head, a floor under your feet.
And home simply means, a place for two souls
From the very first kiss till the juvenile cry
In the nights of Tevet* when the snow falls
And whirlwinds blow.
Four corners for a place of rest.
And to know that in the last hour
Here, at the end, I will close my eyes.

Once there was a home.
(Now, just look at that)
A wagon rolls, far into the world
And on it piled high, rotten mattresses, a cradle
A mirror, a book. and a few mangled chairs,
Pillows and bedding, a flower pot,
And a kitten is running.
It wiggles its tail and meows in fright.

And with this aforementioned procession
Walk behind; man, woman, small child.
They walk behind and pledge:
We shall never, ever forget!
As long as for them there will not be a home
As long as a home, anytime, won't be found
All houses belong to all and to none.
The whole world – one house, and all people,
 Just dear neighbors for us.

4th month of the Jewish calendar

A funeral procession,
Two people follow, a wagon loaded with a home
Some secretly whisper, and some complain.
Some watch with wonder, some with malice stare;
But I understand because I know
Two people are moving somewhere far
To a nicer place, to a better time.

Demonstration

Some people receive a transfer
Others get a bruised fist,
And some, a life – prepared for all risks.
Him – with only one hand.
The war invalid
Did not know what to do.
Something made his tongue stammer,
Something in his mind became confused.
And suddenly he – the right empty sleeve,
Lifted up in the air.
You know:
Every sleeve like that
Is equal to a barrel of a cannon –
Against you!

Make me Understand

Make me understand the difference and aim
Of so much in the world, which to me is not clear.
And mainly: between that which withers, and that which grows,
For I drunkenly sway between life and dream.

For I equally like the blooming and waning
Like a child being questioned by mother and father.
All here is fair. And still more fair, that which is not.
And that which time does not enjoin, is not defiled.

Make me understand the muddled speech
Of old men at their end, while moribund.
And the chattering of his grandchild, who, while full of joy,
Nurses on the milk of his mother's breast.

Make me understand for I don't know for sure.
If the tree is in bloom or covered with snow,
And is not the clear drop of dew on the bloom
Also a tear for that which is doomed?

Make me understand the singing of songs
From which a man eats, and sates his hunger
And the voice of burst jugs, crying to me
And faintly groans when my finger knocks.

Make me understand the difference and aim
Of so much in the world, which to me is not clear.
And mainly: between that which withers, and that which grows
For I drunkenly sway between life and dream.

The Death of my Friend

I walk slowly through the streets.
People pace so quietly and still –
Billboards colorful, holler, sing
What shall I do when they demand, like fields in Tamuz,*
To reap from ourselves the joy, as one would, a ripe fruit?
This early spring morning I stand enchanted, mild and cool.
From where come to us
Such abundance, such wealth?

And suddenly dance advertisements, perfumes,
Brawny athletes, and cackling clowns,
I became overwrought with the voice of my friend,
The mournful voice:
A notice of death, rhyming and dark.

And on that notice, all clear, sharp and cold.
Should I holler and wail in fear and despair?
An athlete on a billboard warns me with a fist.
A clown is ready to stick out his tongue.

A man can yell in the street when he's drunk.
Or a child to weep, when he loses a toy.
A person like me, can just let his head drop
And can only whisper: alas.
Deep within, I begin to wail, as blood-drops pump-out
The minutes, the hours.
I run through the streets, I am chased from walls,
In black letters, like squawking crows.
Oh, how can I, get rid of these shrieking voices?
I cannot out-laugh them like the clown,
Or yell at them like the athlete.
Ever meeting life's face — woe is me,
With the dark weeping face of an obituary.

---

*Month of harvest

Abortion

I did not want to go with her.
But it could not be helped; now I'm standing by the door
Leading from the wait-room at the doctor's place
Eavesdropping in the quietness on what she says:
… Hungry… lonely… unemployed… the need is great.
We sold everything… take… help...

Then it's quiet and I pace, back and forth,
Back and forth.
Standing by the window; I look down to the yard.
I sit, I read and browse, I look at the pictures.
On the table, newspapers and magazines are spread.
One for my dear and pious mother,
A picture on the cover: a child bathes in a tub.
Sprays water, screeches, laughs.
In between, a caption — florid words:
Our single joy in life, a child!
She leaves the room, feverish and pale
And mutters: beloved… my beloved,
Who does she mean? Does she mean — me,
Or her dreamed of, little boy, in the tub of blood?
An hour back she had two lives
Now in her, there is not even one.
We're going down the stairs, I take her by the arm
She's being hauled; not moving on her own
Step by step, there is no end.
And they all lead down, and not one – leads away from this place.

It was spring time outside. Every step in the gardens
The buds had opened, producing white blooms.
Eggs hatched larvae, butterflies and creeping things –
As she does every year — our elated mother nature.

A Woman Speaks

I would like to have a child
There is great joy
In venturing your life
In order to create another.
To have a part in a living creation
With joy, with pain, and with blood!
But I do not have my own apartment
I can't afford a midwife,
A cradle, swaddling.
A liter of milk and a toy.
And I constantly worry and fear
That the first breaths of the child
May not be easy.

The years have remained always gray
But the hair doesn't stay always blond,

And I know:
As many times as a woman bears children –
That many times she's reborn.
Learning to speak – to name people and things
Learning to walk – with small steps
To observe this tremendous earth.
With them she goes every morning to school.
And with them graduates
From one grade to the next.
Becomes a woman again when her daughter,
First menstruates.
Accompanies her son on the first rendezvous,
And stammers out with him, bewildered and bashful
The old timeless words: I love you!
And dances at their wedding, as if it's her own.
And lives her one and only life,

Twice
Three times
Four times,
As many times as the children she's got.

The other night.
I wasn't awakened by a child's cry
I was weeping in my sleep, by myself
My husband left the bed,
Took my hand and woke me:
Why are you weeping – he asked –
What were you dreaming?

I dreamed of a better time;
We already had our own place
A cradle in the corner, diapers in the chest
A liter of milk and a toy
But now it's too late
I'm too barren and old.

Jail

On a Stroll

For David Laser

The prisoners are led on a stroll by the guard
Just like on a leash, one leads a dog.
Sixteen men walk, adrift in the yard
Around two trees and a mound of grass.

Not allowed to talk among themselves,
To say a word, not allowed to wink.
Can only circle one same spot.
As if reciting a secret oath.

One just released from isolation
The darkness was heavy and dense
He's raising his hand to the sun,
He's greeting the light.

A second man had been cleaning the vat
The whole night, in his sleep he gagged.
Now he breaths in, full bottles. And
Staggers drunk with fresh air.

And from the hospital a man just came
His friends gave up on him, but he sees
Hears and walks the earth
Blessing the life he's reclaimed.

And they walk around in the yard
Again and again around the same trees
Until a bird comes flying in
And sits on a limb.

The bird has many-colored feathers
The bird does sing such lovely songs
That the guard wants to catch it
And trap it in his hat.

But the bird flies away
Rising up to the sky
Now it is as small as a dot
And soon it is gone.

Light, air and life – not for everyone.
Oh, to be free, free like a bird!
Sixteen people return to the cell with
Lead on their feet and hands.

Monday Morning

You Collector, Antiquarian!

You,
Who collect — all that is old
That's decrepit and crumbling, and every
Speck of dust from the past
In the closet of your mind.

You,
Who are able to see
From early on,
The object's soul,
When you take it out.

Look around!
See how you strayed!
How instead of living today
You served the bronzed idol
Of yesterday.

You, collector, antiquarian:
Your dusty, dark room leave at once!
Go and see: over sidewalks
Under every stone,
Great things are scattered, abundant
They are not seen by others
No one gathers them up!

What is this with you and the past?
A piece of Napoleon's boot,
A night-shirt from a famed courtesan,
A foot of a king's smashed throne.

And from a holy man, a dry dirty bone.

Ask yourself:
Did you ever own
A hand which was
Torn-off in the plant?
A glance of a child at his labor
So old – like a man, gray and tired?
A bundle of bones of a boy
Who was tortured,
And lived no more, than
Nineteen poor years?

Oh, you collector, antiquarian:
Don't try to revive the dead
With cries and chants
It is all for naught.
Better help those that are fighting
And aching,
And born!

This is the way it Goes

This is how it goes, in the wards of want and toil:
In the morning a man wakes, and sees that on the table
There is still some bread.
Therefore, as once man did, he bows before the sun.
And if he's got a clean bed for his nightly rest
His sleep is laced with lovely dreams.
Should a pregnant woman pass,
Men cast a scornful glance
(For behind every fence there are
Little blue-eyed abandoned young)
The unemployed sense a mounting vigor
Now they move with this unveiled fresh power,
Elevated, purified, amazed each day
In their veins the blood of a new faith sings
Their ascetic wasted faces, light visions
Of a new earthly God.

Premonition, hope, and waiting.
Ears sharply attuned.
Hear the approach of odd intrepid steps
The scent of blood is picked by dogs,
Howling in the night.
Numbers run from bankbooks – like infuriated slaves.
A desire awakens in the train engineer
Out of the rails he's been riding so long.
The prompter now is scared, hearing wondrous things
The actor is off-script, following his own words.
The government minister is afraid of the dancer:
Is she a spy? The king muses; an electric chair —
That's his throne.

The affluent man now walks, barely touching the ground.
It seems to him: a quicker pace, and something would burst.
At night he would like to cuddle up with his gold.

And he cries in his sleep for he sees: the doors
Being crashed, a wild eyed mob rushing in.
Whence come all these people with wonderful deeds?
From all the big cities from the workshops and plants
From coal-mines, sawmills, asylums and jails.
They come to get peace, to settle a debt.
Coal miners at last, see the clear light of day
Sailors, they storm onto dark secure earth.
Porters see them, when the load is removed
And they straighten their backs.
Children at their mother's breast, after sucking
Their own fingers.
Prisoners see it through their window bars
In flying birds,

The day – becomes younger, so much younger
That now it's born to you, you are – its father.

Blind ones, can't you see? Deaf can't you hear?
All paths lead to this place; it's inscribed in the stars.
An hour of pain won't be lost in one day
One tear shall not drop, in the quicksand lost,
All is recalled and all is retold
The day it goes, is the day it comes,
It's already at hand.

Give me Back the Earth Intact

Once there was: a vast whole earth
And came a man, and seized a plot
Enclosed it with a fence and said: it's mine!
And soon, a second came and seized some trees;
Enclosed them with a fence and so declared: mine they will be!
And a third, and a forth, until across the world
There grew: boundaries and ridges, fences and walls.
You can't walk over there, you're not allowed!
This place is for me, there – for you; and for the others?
None!

Once there was a vast whole earth
And people grabbed wide tracts of land
High risers built: here we shall live,
Here we shall dine, sleep with our wives, argue and play.
And they made doors, and on the doors put locks and bolts
And for unwelcome paupers, a peephole.
My bed and my wife, my gold and my closet with clothes
Don't you dare cross my threshold, for you aren't allowed.
This place is for me, there – for you, and for the others?
None!

Once there was a vast whole earth
And people made borders between tracts of land
And at every border: soldiers with rifles and swords.
Don't you dare cross this line, be forewarned!
The fish in the river can swim where they want
The birds are allowed to wander up high
The wind can blow from side to side,
But you – you cannot.
Why? – ask the wind; ask the fish and the birds...
This part is for me, that part is for you, and for the others?
There's no place to go!

And who are the others? – That is us everywhere!
My friend, me and you, and all else around!
For us is the barrier to the orchard and field
For us – the locks on the doors, and for us
The border, between land and land!

In order to buy a small plot from the squire
The peasant had rationed, his children's food.
When he died – none was left for paying his tax.
To pay his rent a neighbor of mine
Sold his pillows and clothes.
After living in there thirty years
Where he knew every nook, and every item was loved.
Where his wedding took place and his children were born.
Where he suffered, rejoiced, where he fought, won and lost –
For missing a payment he was thrown to the street,
Like a bundle of rags.

To cross the border
My friend stole away in the night.
Through the woods, through water and mud.
Seeking work and freedom and bread
But a watchman's bullet brought him to his end.
His blood marked the border of his life, and that
Of two lands.

Now I stand here and ask again and again:
What have you, what have you made of my earth?
You split it with borders, with fences and gates,
Give it back to me whole, free and wide!
It is ours, it is everyone's! Just the way it belongs to us –

After we die.

Give it back, return to me, the earth whole,
With no borders; no gates and no locks!

By the Mountain

It was a Sunday
And a day that's humid, windy and hot;
Like a copper fan, the heavens hung over the city,
Under foot burned the asphalt and broiled
The streets seemed twice as long.
The walls seemed to have moved closer together
The rich left this place long ago
Some to the Zakopaneh and some
To the Carpathians.
From the workers' quarter, the poor, the ill,
Sewer cleaners and tradesmen, factory hands
They too, had managed to leave the town.
But then again, not that far:
To the mountain nearby.

Here they stripped themselves of clothes
And disgracefully lay there for all to see.
A tailor's apprentice with an old man's build
A man of forty, stripped as a babe.
A leg amputee with an unhealed wound.
A mother began to delouse her child's head.
They unbuttoned and then, they re-buttoned themselves.
Wherever there was a blade of grass, they spread
Wherever there was a tree, they stood up and inhaled.
Ten people flocked to a tree.
They extended their hands and cried, "save us, save!"
Ten mouths opened to beg the tree.
And the tree trembled,
            The leaves became jaundiced,
                                and dry.
On one tree, a man saw a squirrel,
And child and adult ran to observe,
And they cheered it on with hoorahs.

And they were ecstatic and wept for joy.
And for a while in the chests, of both old and young
Their hearts, same as the squirrel's joyously thumped.

They rolled in the grass, jumped and ran
Bodies kneaded, merged into one –
Came apart and joined back.
Warmed up in the sun.
Hollered and ranted and screamed,
Refreshed themselves and sweetly sighed:
Gone is the winter with no wood to burn,
With no warm clothes, and hot food,
Gone are the factory dust and fourteen hour work-days
The longing for grass and blue sky
For the wonderful freedom – for the magic of nature
For a whole year, a whole life, for all time!

And it became evening,
Sunset blood pouring over the mountain, it seemed
Like the head of the child whom the mother deloused,
In the grass there is no sight of bees, of insects and flies.
The grass only has fleas and germs.
In the air there's a smell of tobacco and sweat
Everything's breathing so heavy, so hot.

And it became night
Someone begins to quickly dress up:
The shirt, the pants, the shoes
The tailor's apprentice departs with hoarse coughs
The invalid straps the prosthetic leg on.
The worker raps his pipe on a rock,
They rise and begin to go home.

And suddenly there is an unusual calm
(From somewhere, a chirp of a cricket, a bird cries)
And after the silence, over the mountain –

A wild shriek, roaring and strong;
And after the shriek – just a word, as fine and as sharp as a lance:
– Where to?

   Where to?
                  Back, to the filthy unpaved streets in town
With stinking sewers and dank crumbling walls
To which we return, to struggle once more.
If we want to cook – the stoves are broken,
They smoke and they choke,
If we look to the street, the windows are draped with rags
If we want to leave town – the arthritis forbids
And at last, bedbugs bite when we lie down to sleep,
We can no longer endure, enough is enough!

We want an eternal right
For the sun, for the earth, for time;
We don't want to trade off
A whole year for a day and an hour of freedom.
A blade of grass and a leaf in the wondrous outdoors
They do not calm us they excite us more,
And it becomes twice as hard
To return afterwards to this town, to the plant.
Now! Now – not to return there again!
Someplace else, someplace else,
Away from this town.

And I saw:
The mountain, eternally quiet, humble and plain
All at once a volcano became.
And people, like boiling lava, rushing, galloping
Began pouring down,
In the town people moved as if they had wings
   With wretched hollering
            Calling each other,
And through the window panes I could hear the rumble.

Radio

In a cast-off shtetl, every roadway and path
Are covered with snow with storm and with night.
Who could have imagined that just today,
Four people assembled in a home of a friend,
Should turn aside from the road,
And how did it happen that
In their room upstairs, there's a world of sounds.
It is not angels singing by the child's cradle,
God has them secured under a lock;
Daily they must sing his praises thrice, and
Birds do not sing now, this late at night,
They sing only each morning at sunrise,
And haven't found a song for the evening.
They sing to the smallest hillock a prayer
And for the tall skyscraper they silent remain.
They sing praises to trees, and can't understand
When they became telephone poles
And they start singing alone.

From
Greetings From Far (1939)

At the Playground

Children play: someone rolls a hoop, someone
Rides a bike, and someone's on a one wheel cart.
A man goes through on a four wheel cart,
He's missing both legs.
With his hands pushing, onward from below.
Who is it that came?
A new one from a distant street?
Did he, too, come here to play?
The children surround him.
What kind of a child is that? They wonder; and to boot
He has a beard!
Is it of oakum or corn-silk?
They try to pull it off — it's firmly glued. He cries.
But, say, what kind of a four wheel cart is that?
None of them has ever seen or had that type.
They lift him off, and from beneath, they tear that cart away.
A child gives him a jab and flees – catch me!
Now he lies flat on the ground: powerless and lost.
He flaps his arms so strangely, and suddenly it seems that
He has wings!
With all of his strength he picks up himself, lifting his hands,
And flies away over people and roofs, up to the clouds.
For, all people who have no legs, grow wings.

My Child

My child, it may be, you'll be laughing at me –
Six months old, but foreign languages, he already speaks.

I pull out the dictionary from the shelf,
And I search for the words there, and search.

I keep looking till my eyes go blind,
I want, however, to understand my own child.

A whole hour he lies in the crib and cries
Till we can all understand what's on his mind.

Hah-mah, tio-san, he claims with ease;
Seems to me, my child speaks Japanese.

La-leh-loo, he babbles to me from bed
I can swear he was speaking French.

And occasionally, indeed, chee-pei-ping
I am confident, in Chinese he sings.

Again, I take the dictionary from the shelf
And I search for the words and I search.

I once find a similar word and a sound,
But still know not, what he demands.

However, he understands what we say to him,
He can at home recognize all the sounds.

If at home someone weeps – he soon bursts in tears
If someone yells – he too, lets out a scream.

Mother smacks her lips – it starts on the laughter.
She sings a lullaby – his eyes close soon after.

But I, for hours, lie weeping in bed,
For I can understand what lies ahead.

Ah, good people, dear friends, come over!
Know this: I am filled with worry! I ponder,

So many tongues speaks my son when he's small,
How will I understand him when he grows?

I Went With You

You went to look for work
I joined you in your search
Dragging around for hours long
Across foreign streets and squares.

I went with you, stories high
Up staircases, numbered and curved
Unhappily waited by doors, until
Back with an answer you came.

And you returned: ashamed, confused.
And then, I didn't even ask
– They don't need me, they don't,
Your lips quietly sighed.

They don't need you? – I thought of
Sleepless nights in my bed
And how I was faint and sad
That for a minute you were not there.

I have gently uttered in song,
And relayed, but was silenced
And lost,
Going with you in your search for work.

The Seamstress

By the sewing machine stitching a dress
The bobbin is getting thinner and sparse
It will be a skeleton in just a trice.

The day was long, a summer's day;
An hour unwound,
An hour more, and it's late at night.

Needle, needle! Where do your sisters go?
The old broken needles, where do they go?
Of such old needles, my back is full.

After work – they rest in bed. They sleep as one
Next to the sewing-machine, call out, remembering
Young age, dance on my shoulders, my sides.

Hush now, calm down! – This dress must, nevertheless,
Be ready at dawn. Even the clock on the wall is asking
The whole time: Rea-dy? Rea-dy? Rea-dy?

But her shoulders drop lower; her head falls on her breast.
She dozes off. Slowly the dress slips onto the floor.
In her sleep she is frightened, tries to wrench out her arms
And it seems to her that she's awakened herself and sews on.
The clock wants to wake her, it rings; one, two, three.
But she's not waking up.

The clock breaths heavily: it can no longer ring;
It must wait a whole hour.
Tranquil in bed, lies a full white moon,
And on a stool sits dreaming and bent,
This sleeping seamstress, young and pale.

A Letter to China

From a faraway country a letter I wrote,
To Su-Li, the coolie, in Shanghai:

In China I wasn't, not even a day,
However I'm sure, that there is such a man.

I see him run across the streets of Shanghai,
He pulls the rickshaw and heavily pants.

He's ever weary but it's his consolation:
Each drop of sweat will turn into rice.

And the sweat is dripping, and it seems that soon
Of weakness he'll sink-down and collapse.

If he only knew that right now
A mail-carrier, is bringing a letter.

No one around turns to look at him
But somewhere far, someone thinks of him.

But the letter will go for three months or longer
Until one day, it will be returned.

It will be stamped: 'unknown address',
Though all over the land, all know who he is.

For a burden to carry – they go to him.
For sewing a dress they seek him out.

Someone breaks the law – he is harassed.
If two people fight, he's a part of that fight.

And maybe like me, he too, sends a letter,
Across the sea, to the lonely and sad.

But his letter, one finds, is also returned
The address on it, no one understands.

They do not know that their race is vast,
Yellow skin is found in each house and hut.

Not the yellow of birth, but such that hunger
Has wilted and struck their young insides.

And in the pit they are both, Israel and Su-Li
People fear that one day, they may long to be free.

But this you must know: in all homes one can find:
Unopened letters that were sent back.

Who will collect the yearnings, sent 'round the world,
That have no address and must return home?

Oh song, a mail-carrier be!
Find the lonely, the sad and tired for me.

Talk to them, tell them: in each country and town
Lie letters unopened in everyone's drawer,

And all who've been waiting tired for long,
Should answer their letter – in song!

In the Pawn Shop

A man stands in line in the pawn shop
The proprietor asks:
What did sir bring in to pledge?
The man hears:
A silver bell –
A laughing child
A gasping hungry cry.
Answers the man: I've brought only myself.
Yourself? The proprietor is a little bemused,
Never before he'd heard such a tale.
He observes the man through a monocle; no,
Not of silver and gold, but of skin and bone.
He motions dismissively with his hand,
– A man – we don't deal in such
Cheap merchandise…

Travel Song*

Come into our houses and you'll see:
Valises filled with clothes.

Bags on the bedding and maps
With cities, underlined in red,

And walking sticks and knapsacks
In case we have to walk.

The little notebooks with addresses,
Are they wishes or greetings?

With the dead in the graveyard parting,
We shed the last tear.

So much we had here at the graveyard
And such a small part of life.

Now, when in the hallway, footsteps we hear
We jump with a start, that's it, at last!

Quickly, kissing your wife and child,
And with your hands grab a suitcase and box.

We want to go away from here!
We think, mountains can't move,

If we were mountains –
Each of us would be a volcano!

We want to be far! We spell it out:
— Trees are stuck in one place – that's so hard.

If we were trees — we would yield
The bitterest fruit!

Travel, travel, we are nervous and wild
It's so crowded and stuffy in here.

We live through an earthquake each day,
– It tumbles our homes and our dreams,

Every night I see:
Lit-up stations, trains going away.
But dawn comes, and
The rails cannot be found.

Every night we have wondrous hope.
Ships sailing to countries devoid
Of winter and frost, but morning comes
And all ships go under.

* See a different version of this poems on page 115. I considered the
poems different enough, to justify presenting both versions.

Once did Love...

Once did love to evening long
To fetch the white moon from the sky,
Now: at noon beneath the sun
Bodies flowing, burning hot!

By the river-dam they wish
To extinguish wild desire
A wonder in a wonder! See:
Among the waves do flicker fires!

They want to cool the torrid blood
In the forest, in the shade,
But under trees lust burns still stronger
Than inside the house.

The ugly ones date one another
The hunchback looks for the deformed
The half-witted meets the fool,
No virgin will be coming home.

Soon, the whole forest in fever
The shrubs, the grass, the trees,
Squirrels, crickets, hares.
The birds, the lizards, and bees.

All loved caressed and paired,
On trees in the weeds, in the foliage
The God Pan, to a cave crawled of shame,
And the opening he closed with a boulder.

In the old Notebook

In the old notebook from the shtetl
It is written so:
At first there were straw-huts of peasants and
A Jewish blacksmith and a tavern by the road
Then one more Jewish store – selling fuel and salt.
A shoe-maker a tailor, and then a whole association
Real houses showed with shakes and shingles.
Then they glued up a small post with a plank
And a hand point with a finger: a shtetl!
In the old notebook it is written:
How lived there a certain Haimy-livin'.

Once he strayed in the said countryside
By the field-gate where the roads fork apart.
And suddenly saw the post with the plank
And the hand that points with a finger: a shtetl.

A shtetl? How come? Until now there were just,
Rabbits and wind in free fields of grass.
He had to travel through each country road
And spend the night, under the stars.
Could this be true? One might as well —
Sniff this oddness out. And at dawn, arriving
In the shtetl,
Three wagons filled with all kin and relations
The family lodged;
Stepmother squeezed into the little straw house
Grandma cared for – in the poor street behind.
The sister longingly, paired with a spinster
Old grandpa in the den by the stove.
The grandchild joyously, in the new rich man's house
But for the uncles and brothers in-law
It was all too scant: in the market today they are
Still fighting over the store.

Like the shtetl's ruler Haimy-livin' rolled,
But in one place he was overcome
A mighty thing, his greatest fright:
The road that led straight to the graveyard.

Poems Featured in two Different Books

The nine following poems in this section were first featured in 'Monday Morning' (1937), and then in 'Woe and Wander' (1950). See also 'Translator's Note'

Childhood

My Mother's Early Morning Walk

Has anyone seen, my mother in the morning, on her way
To the store, to buy some buckwheat, bread or rice?
Perhaps no one has, for, who would pause to observe
An old Jewish woman, skin and bones, in old dress
And non-matching shoes? And since I'd like her to be
Remembered, I will here describe her morning walk.

Mother goes to the grocery store, and worriedly
Ponders on which excuse – for borrowing to use.
The grocer yesterday, did already warn: that
With no money at hand, she can't knock on his door,
And it means, days and weeks of empty stomachs,
And we must sell the mirror, the desk and bed covers.

So mother turns this way and that, before the store.
It seems to me: any moment she will be down
On all fours, wild like a beast — ready to pounce
And everything tear to cool her rage, but mother
Does not. Powerless, meek, mother stands still
Close to the store and she is peeking in.

She sees: bread on the shelves, sugar in bags
And butter in tubs. the dial is drunk, scales
Dancing with joy. And she sees her apartment, the kitchen
Cold, the empty pots, five people sit with downcast heads,
And she says: I'll go in, try my luck once again.
And she walks to the store – and then…she returns.

She goes back home again, she is now in the yard.
Stealthily climbs the stairs to the flat, and she stands,
Puts her ear to the door, hears the cries

Of hunger from people and utensils alike, and her
Head hangs lower, and her face is sadder
And so she walks to the store, one more time…

Endnote:

You, passerby, who in early morning
Go through our streets, and meet a pale woman –
Know this: she's my mother,
And even though on her face it shows that she
Intends to commit, a dark sinful deed, indeed
A crime, she is only preparing to borrow some food:
A loaf of bread, a pound of potatoes or rice…

The Sick Father and his new Shoes

My father lay sick in his bed, and under the bed
Were his new shoes.

Life and death waged war in my father's chest
Breathlessly gazing at the spittoon, he knew:
On the sand lay his expectorated breast.
And the lightness from our home disappeared.
The glasses for the Sabbath's wine were gone,
And the number of bitter medicine-bottles increased.
If a child laughed, father's stare would stab –
Like a shard of glass, mangle that laugh into fright.

And as life and death battled in my father's chest,
Winter struggled with spring;
Snow was falling – rain pouring down.
The putrid dampness invaded all body parts.
In the morning mother has to go to the store
And then the brother – to slave at work.
And none of us had shoes that were whole.

So we thought: if father's just the same, sick in bed,
Let someone take his shoes for a stroll
And the thief shuffled softly across, and
Father gasping for air, became worse,
His eyes are closed but he hears, and as if
Whispering, pleading:
– Let them lie… I will need them… my shoes…

Father thought to himself:
On account of his shoes, he would longer survive
Let each shoe be an envoy to God.
But if – God forbid! they were taken away–
He would be lost, and never get up.

Father's bed is empty.
In his breast death won against life,
On the other hand, in the street, spring, like a hero
Against the winter has won, Passover in the world!
I wear my father's shoes, they are too large.
But mother says: a child grows up!

A Holiday in Town

Today, it is a holiday in town
An early morning, like a wooly white lamb bowing at
God's feet.
The cloisters are swimming like ships
On blue oceans of sacred song.
Mother Maria bedecked with wreaths,
And unlike always, regrets that her Jesus
In diapers, is holding her all to himself,
And she cannot pick up all the street children onto her lap.
The louts feel that their money, is burning them like
Judas Iscariot,
The pig slaughterer's, blood-red trembling hands
Are bleached.
Over everyone's head like halos float holy rays of light
For today it is a holiday in town.
It is a holiday in town.
An evening like a black bull running wild.
Meanwhile, in the taverns broke out a war
They vomit and — they urinate in the street.
Soldiers trying to hire, a sixteen year old girl,
They want to have her together, but she hesitates
Eight men are a little too much.
From the bridge to the water a drunk fell down,
In a dark side-street, some youths robbed,
And strangled a man, and one
Chased his pregnant wife to the street.
On her body one can even see the bruises.
Because today, it is a holiday in town.

The new Man

Four men in the tavern, it is the twelfth hour.
The alarm rings, fire! But there is no help.

As one would drown a meowing cat,
They drown their sorrows in wine.

They drink one glass after the other
Until the publican, waddles over

And says: my friends! I beg of you, don't laugh.
Today I propose to make a new man!

Four people raise their glasses, and yell:
Bravo! Bravo! The proposition's fine!

The first one bows: my present is useless and useful
At once, I present the new man with my own glass eye.

The second one says: here is my large gift
I present the new man with my own false teeth.

And then says the third: let it among us be known:
I present the new man with my rubber arm.

And the fourth one (his words roll like shelled seeds)
I present the new man with my wooden feet.

Now the publican calls: and for the new man,
I present as a gift: my fat abdomen.

Four people raise their glasses and shout:
A man! Let there be… a new man!

And at once they are quiet, as if by a slaughterer's blade
There stands the new man bearing his fangs.

They tremble in fear and disgust and moan,
How will they get rid of this frightful ghost?!

They pounce on him, fling his body around!
Each trying to kill his own trait that he loathes,

But soon they are shamed and do understand:
This is what each wants to do to his friend.

Five men in the tavern, their heads to the table are sinking
And weep out the wine that they finished drinking.

A Hungry Dwelling

The kitchen –
Dreams like an old woman:
– Oh, if someone wishes to
Take pity:
A pail of coal,
A sack of wood,
To warm one's olden bones.

The pots and pans hang on the walls,
Their mouths are open wide,
They cry:
Abate our hunger,
Extinguish our thirst
We would like some potatoes,
A spoonful of borscht!

The beds are piled so high with covers
They cannot see what's happening
Around them.

But the people are silent.
They are so fearfully silent
In their pain.

The Secondhand Suit

With money I saved, I bought a suit.
Second hand – from one of the stores.
Whoever wore it before as new – I don't care
Why should I trouble myself with his name?

I removed the stains with benzene
And the missing buttons – sewed on.
I looked in the mirror and saw my face,
Smiling, delighted with joy.

And I would have liked in my jacket's lapel,
A flower; small, fragrant and red.
But in the pocket I found a receipt,
And a smell of a hospital and death.

The pants began to wrinkle anew,
The spots on the jacket – came back;
It was not a light colored suit, but black death
Which engulfed my trembling heart.

And here I'm alone, as if facing a stranger
An eternity passed in that speck of time
And I thought: when I spit out now
I spit just like he did – with blood!

The old rag Picker

In his older years, what more can he find
But an old crumpled suit gnawed by mice,
A calendar with some of the pages missing
An unpaid bill from a grocery store.

Even in his nicest dreams he can't see new clothes.
And no longer remembers himself as a child.
Wrinkles can be – ironed out of a suit.
But for a wrinkled face there is no cure.

Till one day, it's death, the eternal rag picker
As *he* does now, will go through town,
And call out with a hoarse smothered voice:
Old things! Old things! Bones, I buy bones!

And slowly a door of a cellar will swing,
And free of charge the corpse handed out,
The bones drained of strength and marrow and blood
In a small dirty sack of hide.

Jail

The sun Rises in the West

Till now I've never heard of this
And never read it anywhere,
Of such a land wherein the sun
Should truly rise in — from the west.

If someone with this news had come
I would have surely laughed at him
Till I was told this on a day
When I was thrown in jail.

And I observed: all windows there
Were facing west and only
An early evening ray can strike them
When the sun would set.

And it is not a fairy tale
Nor an ancient dream
A person, as you see, can change
The sun's daily routine.

Our sun rises in the west
Rises – when she sets.
When shadows creep from every crack
And we're prepared to sleep the night.

Past the horizon, hiding,
Giving us a final laugh
To some she says – good morning!
To us – she says good night.

Bread

Here there are great masters
Who with their hands do make
Things which they have known
Outside these prison gates.

It is a marvel to recount, for
They, from bread will craft:
Tobacco pipes, figures for chess
And people, casks and birds.

But it is a daily mess:
In prison there is not enough
And creating without bread,
That, nobody can.

What else can we all do?
We redeem ourselves of death
By kneading out of bread
A person or device.

Just bread, just give us bread,
And the world will bless
Life inside the men
And with man – this life.

The next ten poems were originally featured in 'Greetings From Far' (1939) and then in 'Woe and Wander'(1950)

Mother Tells

Now children, I come from the market in the city,
That you haven't seen the market, is a pity;
Such abundance and bounty you've never seen
Both meat and fish, fruit and provisions,
It seems there's enough for all to share
But I stand at the market like a dummy, and I stare.

If I bought herring, I couldn't buy bread.
If I bought cabbage l couldn't buy meat.
Gitel, she wants liver,(what does she think!)
And Berele cries: buy me an apple to eat!
The few pennies I have, I squeeze in my hand,
And I stand at the market like a dummy, and I stare.

A bossy lady jostling through the crowd,
– Why stand you in the middle? You block the path!
And with rigid reprove a Jew is cursing:
The store is for buying, not for dreaming!
They yell and they push me thither and back
But I – I stand like a dummy and I stare.

In the landladies' buckets the fish die dumb
In the landlady's pockets the summer is done
With beets and apples, tomatoes and cabbage,
The rich summer bounty is just for her rummage
And the sack and pitcher, the larder and jar
But I still stand there like a dummy, and I stare.

It's all down to one choice: a flower pot?!
No fruit, no meat, no cabbage no honey?
I buy it from the Jew, with my last few pennies.
Now see, how beautifully the flowers are blooming
One flower isn't even, ready for picking
But why do you all stand like dummies and stare?

We Were Children

I recall: we were children, and
Each year winter came:
A winter with frolicking blizzard and chill
When like a graveyard, the shtetl is still.

Once… as children we still dreamed
Of such summer, that always brings:
Cherries, apples and plums,
And we longed for a spring eternal.

We dreamed of a wonderful marvel:
Behind a window there would be
An acacia — forever blooming, and
A blue fragrant lilac on the table.

Until we all, at one time hatched a plan:
To steal matches from our mothers
Light them up together outdoors,
Melt the snow and ice with the flames.

And the night was dark, and the night was cold,
Three children not knowing of any danger.
Lighting matches, flicking them through the air
Burning holes in the face of the frost.

In the shut homes by their stoves
Warm up the grownups and the old,
But in a raw winter night, three children
Wish to warm up the entire world!

But the blizzard won't calm
And the frost does linger, and if
The matches in the box misfired
They could even, burn a finger!

Did we warm up the world?
I cannot recall, but I can certainly swear,
That for us, the matches were lovelier
Than the God-lit stars in the sky.

The Lost Ball

How did the ball disappear?
All played with it a moment ago
Here It was lying in everyone's hands,
And there it was seen by the boys.
But suddenly – it flew like a bird –
Disappeared from everyone's view!

And where did the ball really go?
No one knows where it dropped
Perhaps it went over a fence?
Perhaps on a roof of a house?
And perhaps in a tree or the shrubs?
Moyshe! Yosel! Mendel! Let's climb up!

The children search for the ball,
Meanwhile, the night slowly falls.
They are tired of running around
Hunger is gnawing at their little hearts
But suddenly: what a surprise!
The children watch and wonder:

The ball is among the clouds!
It is burning, in the west, going down.
They have thrown the ball so high
Did God too, want to play and took it
Up there? A moment more and it's gone!
God wanted it all for himself!

One child bitterly cries:
 – I'm afraid to go home,
My father will punish me
And will moralize.
God! Give back the ball!
He cries, and with him
All the children cry.

Waterfall and Mountain

In the valley by the waterfall, a man gets photographed.
And on the mountain, by the rocks he wants
To bond with water and mountain — his ephemeral life.

The waterfall is never tired, its movement:
Cheerfully charging the rocks, angrily foaming.
Drooling with joy in victorious uproar.

The mountain is never riled, it is tough:
Should the rain or the snow or the storm rage –
It remains powerful, calm. A mute monument
To its own might and strength.

Cries out the man: waterfall, give me your vigor!
Begs the man: mountain, give me your peace!
But the waterfall doesn't know of giving and gifts.
It is used to flow over, and carry away and seize.

And the mountain asks: what are you looking for
On my perilous, powerful shoulders? For peace?
You can get peace only, under a small mound of earth.

On the Mountains

I had always thought: heaven has no end
Now I am to it – ascending with no wings.

I had always thought: but I am the one
Who back to earth brings heaven down.

What is joined in song: planet, star and earth,
With potato and bread – shoes and bed.

Now I see: more than the loveliest song can do
It is a mountain that binds the two.

From mountains move vapors – billowing smoke,
Uniting with clouds in the heavenly nights.

Up in the clouds all is engulfed;
Of the same earth, the heavens rise.

And to no avail have the pious conceived
To break heaven from earth, body from mind,

With knapsack and boots, body and soul
I'm in heaven alive.

As a child in my most devout moment of prayer
I never felt so close to God.

Convalescence

O man! O son! O tree!
Look: how he barely drags himself
For the first time, in the street
Receive him as he is.

On his sick bed
He always spoke in his fever to me
And silently dreamed and longed
To man! To son! To tree!

To the hospital he went
The body cut, with needles prodded
Oh, so many times!
And bathed through long nights
In cold sweat and heat, and
It's you who he torridly loved.

Now as he comes out
Still fighting for you,
Show that you remember him
And long for him too.

Welcome, thank him from your heart,
Son! Ruddy your paleness
In your eyes light the light
Your body — that had already felt
The stiffness of death,
Live, warm up!

O tree! Take from leaf and branch
And put breath in his breast
Freshness of blood and bloom,
Pour your sap in his blood, and
Make him again younger and bright.

The Birth of Hershele of Ostropol

The mother to the neighbors would complain:
This is the eighth time she is pregnant, but
This time, it is really strange. During
Pregnancy one craves a pickle,
An onion or some cabbage, but she — how odd,
She craves a bowl of sweetened carrots.

And lo, there came the time of labor,
Around her bed — grandma and the women had
Prepared to hear the first cry of the child:
Ay-ay, ay-ay, like a new born would do
But of a sudden: hee-hee, hee-hee, a laughter –
The women passing out of fear.

For crying out loud! What kind of child is this,
It must be, he's possessed by demons!
The good Jews give him amulets and charms
The quacks put on him coins, and against
The evil eye, extinguish coals,
However, nothing seems to work.
The mother isn't sure what ails him,
And brings him milootin-mitzikootin,
She boils some herbs and roots for drinking
And his body rubs with ointments.
But of help there is no sign —
On Hershele's face there's still a smile.

Mother never used to fear:
Should a child get chickenpox, the measles
Scarlet fever, or even the English Malady*
With all she is familiar, and for all there is

---

* Rickets (lack of vitamin D)

A cure. But now with him — the neighbors must be right
An old man coughs —— a baby has to cry.

But Hershele, he doesn't know and doesn't care
He wishes no more than to play and play,
He goes outdoors and runs around,
Plays pranks, one worse than the other
His mom bewails her suffering and fate
But with Hershele, rejoice
All the people of Ostropol.

The above poem was originally featured in 'Woe and wonder, but is
included here with the other Poems about Hershele.

The Death of Hershele of Ostropol

Hershele's household is dumb and pale.
They thought: will this jaundiced face
With a new smile, not ever shine again?
And Hershele will speak: heh – heh you fools,
You thought that Hershele surrendered,
Not so fast, not in death's stinking life! ...
And he'd shake his head with beaming joy
That old man, Hershele, fooled you again...

And so, mournful is the house and
Equally, prepared to smile.
But suddenly they see — a shadow
On the mirror spreading like a veil.
The last smile on his face was stiff
Like a cold bird on frozen ground,
Lamenting that comfort can't be found
For, the one who gave them comfort, now lay still.

And eerily and silently, deep in the night
Rabbi Bruchel, from dark dreams, woke with a start
The wind in the window extinguished a candle
And Hershele did not rekindle the light.
The Rabbi soon grasped what had occurred
And lit a candle, for him who passed.
He whispered: blessed be the True Judge, bless be
The Creator! But at heart, like an owl in a ruin
Melancholy struck.

The Tombstone of Hershele of Ostropol

Here lies Hershele, Hershele of Ostropol
Body fed with potatoes, kasha and borscht
And dressed in torn and tattered clothes.
His whole life a weakling — by miracles maintained
That wife of his, had a wretched dark fate
Here lies Hershele; Hershele of Ostropol.

Elijah the Prophet indeed does come
To arbitrate the rabbis' rift
But each day increases the gold of the rich.
And the more the rabbis study the Torah,
The more they sink in gloom, and the more
The rich count their gold, the more
They are scared of thieves.
But he went around with a joyous faith,
And who would have robbed his golden smile
When it was there for all — free to share?

Here lies the wise Hershele under a stone
Hershele who stole away from heaven
To serve melancholy with a drink of joy
God missed him so much in the sad Garden of Eden,
And plagued him with hardship so that he'd quit earth
But the more he suffered, the bolder he turned.
Until like an old hunting dog he gave in —
May his joy be bound with our gloomy being.

The Last Owner

The dog lost his master somewhere
And strayed in the street all alone
Of a sudden, he saw him on a tramway car
And barked and cried for joy,

He leaped but failed to reach,
And soon lay covered with blood
With humility his paw he stretched,
For his last owner — for death!

1929

Don't Trust the Spear... (From 'King Saul')

Don't trust the spear too much, my love:
The spear alone will never save you.
For just the same — my love is brave,
And renders you in battle grand.

And the battle you'll survive,
My love will be your armor;
Hatred leads you to the war,
And love will lead you back victorious.

Don't trust your arrows much, my love:
By themselves they will not save you,
My love, too — is brave and strong,
Defeating hatred far and wide.

From the battle you'll return,
My love will be your armor;
Hatred leads you to the war,
And love will lead you back victorious.

Don't trust too much the sword, my love:
The sword alone will never save you
My love, too — is like a hero,
Chasing hatred from the land.

From the battle you will rise,
My love will be your armor;
Hatred leads you to the war,
And love will lead you back victorious.

Woe and Wander

Author's Preface

In the book are presented poems which have for the most part, been written during and after the war. I have also given a certain space to poems written before the war, since my two last books did not come out to the readers. The penultimate book "Greetings from far" was published several months before the German-Polish war and the latest *Premonition and reality* – several weeks before the German- Russian war.

Surely it is hoped that a writer would come out with a book whenever he has collected the proper amount of poems. (When a writer does not write poems for, so to say 'eternity', he writes them firstly for his own time.) That said opportunity I didn't have, and the reader would have to imagine the time when they were written.

Even though the poems had been written during a span of twenty years, I arranged them in divisions. Those, which remain unclassif-ied' I put in a group titled 'From various times'.

Many of my poems had stayed out of print. I will, now give them a place between covers. I would like to mention the two great lost poems: 'I invite you to a masquerade ball' and 'Uriel Acosta' and furthermore, poems which I only remember their names, and other ones which even their names I have forgotten.

The people whom I had previously forgotten, I will now mention in the following poems.

Israel Aszendorf

Letters

The Gothic letters are —
Prickly like daggers,
Pointy like spears.
The Latin letters —
Barrels, filled with ruddy wine.
The Yiddish letters aren't so drunk
Of blood or wine — just
Squared and hunched and nailed
Like the fate of my people.

Childhood

A Ladder Leads up to the Attic

A ladder leads up to the attic and, I rush
And climb on it so many times each day.
New worlds unfold before my eyes
Here hang a shirt and towel on a line
Here is a splurge almost as merry as Passover
There runs a mouse chased by a cat,
There, the caged hen lays an egg (cock-a-doodle!?)
And I run down the street, to bring
The news, the whole kit and caboodle
And comes the rain – I move, hear with delight
I spring and sing – from the roof-tops, and still
I marvel and, more and more, I cannot stop.

But, sometimes I am awake in bed
And see the terror in the dark of night.
From the attic ladder now descends
An old horned devil with a beard ablaze
An evil trident in his hand.
A hoard of demons, bearded like some goats
Each one is hanging from his neighbor's tail
Each one is sticking out his tongue.
They come toward my bed to scare me
I strain across the blanket in one stride
I hear each rap and clap within my heart
Bang – bang, bang-bang. It's springing out
And suddenly I do cry out.
The mother wakes and asks: what's that?
What's that my child? What's that befell?
I stammer: fiends… they are… it's here…
So mother's standing down next to the bed.
Already a young man – and scared of ghosts,
She carries me into her bed and I,
I cling to her and fall asleep at once.

Childhood

Now I am close to my thirtieth year,
And it's hard to remember my youth,
It comes for a moment at night in my sleep,
From faraway wandering-roads:
I take it with joy, like a mute
Who had just recovered his voice.

But there, still lives my good old mother.
My youth by her side, kept in my heart.
I'm going home to visit her now
There, is my life's wonderful part.
She is mothering me, I grow and learn
She's enabling my youth.

But today it is fall, and a gray rainy day
In the street I encounter a small crying child.
The eyes red of crying, the cheeks are pale
Through foreign streets he wandered alone
Asking me to take him home
But his address he doesn't know.

And I, who was going to see my mother –
Remained standing, and at once understood
From the meeting, the mystery and sign:
By her, I will no more encounter my youth.
The door which her trembling hand opened,
I will no longer find.

And childhood lies in all places,
Looking at me for kind words and protection.
It will no more appear – diffusing at evening
Through my mother's drained voice,
But early morning a head of a child
Will lift in the air, and call me — father!

Praise to a Swallow

Autumn

The dismal rainfall writes its crooked letters
On brown and yellow leaves: summer's gone.
The wind spies on every door and face.
People lift umbrellas like black flags.
Summer's bounty lies in sacks and jars,
In the album — beauty of nature and of women.

Praise to a Swallow

Oh swallow, I will now sing your praise:
Between the rocks the eagle seeks his rest.
The nightingale – on tree and bush, but you –
Beneath a human roof.

You flew away in autumn, and how far!
But from afar you long for home,
And on your wings you bring the spring,
Beneath a human roof.

And so do I; I, who must wander on dirt roads:
In field, in forest, mountain, vale.
Forever and again I tremble as I stand:
Beneath a human roof.

Mountains

There, tower the giant mountains, far,
But to me, quite different than they always seemed.

All around, as far as one can see it's green.
But they — they carry snow upon their rims.

They are now — no longer still as stones,
But light and loose and hanging clean,

As if they would exhale the earth to heaven,
And soon be swimming with the clouds.

To the Mountains

I have addressed the mountains so:
 – Oh mountains! After endless wandering
And toiling long, I'm resting here and fleeing
From worries' wrinkled hands.

They, however, recognized me in a draft of wind,
The footprints here already traced,
Oh, put yourself between us,
Protect and save me, like a fortress wall:

Through the day the mountains saved me
But at night the worries weren't put to rest.
They dug a tunnel underneath the peaks,

And in the morning when I woke,
The gate was open all the way, and soon,
On the threshold all the worries stood.

To a Sapling

Today's a day in mid-October,
But it is still as warm as May,
A lilac sapling's standing naked,
But prepared to bud afresh.

So small a sapling it's a crime!
I'd bet it's one or two days old.
Here shines on you a heaven's star,
Here, drips on you a dismal plague.

And in your ear the wind does sigh
Much praise and gentle touch:
Don't trust his love, for it won't last —
Here it howls and whips you wild.

You will lose your leaves at last
And there will come a time as such:
In your despair – a raven black,
To you will be a guest beloved.

But in the time of great despair
Do not forget the coming spring,
And under burdens of white snow
Bring out the one blue lilac dream.

The Withered Branch

What says the withered branch
That spring had left forlorn?
It is hanging silent, stiff,
A miracle won't help.

But still within himself he comfort finds –
I could still – become a stick,
And help a man who's blind
To feel the stepping of his feet.

And fare to be consumed,
Burning in a pyre.
My warmth will be at hand
For men to further live.

But branches that turn green,
Of nothing now they think:
They're kissed by every bee
And do what they may not.

They think: that blossom will
Now hang off them for good,
And will not have to bring
Into this world, a fruit.

You

You, who give all fruit their shape:
The plum should be, larger than the cherry,
And larger than both —
The apricot.
The apple should be round and the pear
Wide bellow and smaller above.
You also give the form to my song.

You who give all things their voice:
The whirlwind should be stronger than the breeze
And stronger than both —
Is the storm.
The cloud should loudly thunder, and
A fountainhead quietly murmur,
You also give the rhythm to my song.

You who give your essence to all creatures:
The eagle — talons and beak, the elephant
Its trunk. The wolf — his teeth, and armor to
The porcupine,
You also give the power to my song.

From various times

Breath

Breath is like a quiet man
Who smoothly slinks into a home.
He enters in, then out he goes
You do not notice him at all.

But now, when plane is decked with frost
White death on lake and woods,
And also will my heart make cold —
With my own eyes, I see it too.

Ah breath! I keep you for a flash
Against the cold, the frost and death
I am alive: I am, I am!

Like a victory-sign that soars!
Death will readily not come —
I shall resist! Till my last breath...

The Kitten and the Worm

The seventh of April
In the antiquarian's window
A kitten sitting still, and
Fondled by the sun.

The worm is slinking in a book.
The book is old and cold,
Yellow and dank.
It crawls and revels:
Oh how clever
Oh how much power
How much holiness
In every page!

It speaks and gnaws and can't
Be satisfied.

This kitten though
Sits peacefully and pleasantly —
His feet are folded under,
He sweetly shuts his eyes.
But suddenly he opens up his mouth,
And yawns
And lazily replies:

Oh worm, you fool!
I'd give up all you want:
The wisdom, power, holiness
Of all the books — for
One warm ray of light
In winter time.

Beards

My grandfather, uncle and father,
They all had generous beards
Like foliage of olden oaks.

Hid one from the others his sorrow
Behind his beard, the black.

Hid one from the others his love
Behind his beard, the blond.

Hid one from them his grief and rage
Behind his beard, the red.

Grief, love and rage
Had in their beards nestled
Like storms in dense woods,

But my face against each peril stood;
Came sorrow love and rage
Plowing my face with troughs,

And so, exposed I stand against all threats
With my sorrow love and rage,
On my open defenseless face.

Nothing Different

Already midday,
But empty stand
Pot and bowl
In our home
Still nobody
Had breakfast.
Mother's looking for
What to sell
In the cupboard.
But I - I sit and search
A word and a metaphor
For my song.

Rebukes me the mother:
How can you peacefully sit
With your rhymes ?

Oh mother, know
And listen too:
I don't do anything much different
Then you do.
If your life is hard
You weep
Before the Sabbath candle-lights.
You pour out your heart
To a neighbor.
And for those such as myself,
It is destined
To argue cry and fret
With the twenty two Jewish letters
Of the alphabet.

Travel Song*

We're sitting hunched over the maps
And looking for new lands to reach.

After all, there must be somewhere that is safe
For our parents, wife and child.

In the graveyard to the dead we bade farewell,
We gave them our final tears.

We, in the graveyard left so much
And such a small fragment of life.

And far we want to be, we think,
The trees stand still, how hard it is:

If we were trees –
How bitter our fruit would be.

We're looking at the mountains and we think:
They know how not to move away.

If we, God forbid, turned to mountains –
We'd all, for sure become volcanoes.

But the mountains stay serene
And the trees, they grow sweet fruit.

For us, however, earth can only tremble
And destroy our homes.

Railway stations every night we see in dreams
The trains are going, going, but at dawn

When we get up, when we look for the trains
It's hard to even find the rails.

Each night in our dreams we see:
One by one the ships are sailing,

With music, song, and banners stirring
But at dawn – all ships are sinking.

---

* See a different version of this poems on page 67. I considered the poems different enough, to justify presenting both versions.

Love

By Your Side

Sleeping by your side
I saw again,
How, when lying next to you,
We meet in dreams again.

How sad I woke at dawn,
And almost thought
I was here quite alone
But once awake, again I've found you.

Oh say: is reality resumption of dream
Or dream — that of what's real?
Who knows? But to me it's clear:
You're mine in both.

And always will my eyes behold,
How you connect, oh woman,
My reality and dream, like earth and heaven
Are connected by a rainbow.

Expectation

You have escaped to a foreign land
But in the street each day I see
A woman in the distance dressed
Like you: same shape, same gait –
Forgetting that the distance now
Between us is so great,
Hastily to her I go.

And she really is a stranger
Then to myself I mutely say:
Go home, and at the door
She waits for you. But then
I do not find you and I say
Do not torment yourself.
She had just gone out for a while,
The evening-bread was what she lacked.

And you don't come, it's late at night,
I shove myself into the corner
Of the bed, and making room
For you, because I still believe
You still could come, and gently move
So that I wouldn't, couldn't feel
That you are lying by my side.
And you come not – so let the dream
Bring you to me, as far as you may be.

Footprint

I used to walk alone with yearnings
Looking for the footprints on the road
To the garden, where we both
Many times had met.

How often now, old streets are newly built;
It is a marvel, and the foreign streets
Close-by and cozy, like
It's where we lived.

The streets have led us somewhere
Like we were following a clue,
And the last one us delivered
To the trees and garden gate.

Quickly over us the trees had lowered,
Bent their heavy limbs,
And the birds on them were ordered
to see and hear — and to be mute.

Yes, now we're silent too. Warm kisses,
Lips are firmly pressed, and
Stronger than the bark around a tree it's
You, I do embrace.

But every move we make, does
Fill the shadows with more envy.
Why won't you allow the joy —
Of a pale and withered neighbor?

Now I go on searching for old tracks
Stray away, becoming lost;
I'm led from one street to another
Until I lose them all.

All have left now, as you did
I'm standing shamed and lost.
No more to the garden I shall go,
For I am fearful of it now:

Once I went there all alone,
Stood beneath our tree,
And every jealous shadow
Then was mocking me...

To a Child

Oh child, you long to be
As strong as I would be.
I await a note from her,
And you, await a sign.

In every note a woman
Extends to me her hand
And you — with every sign
Conquer the earth.

After each note, it seems
that she is really mine.
And you – will be a king
Of that far, far land.

Oh fate be merciful,
I beg you so:
Do not let it be lost:
For a child — his kingdom
And for me — a wife.

You Weep

You weep through my dream
In a song:
I am on a tree
Still just a bloom.
So you had robbed
My hot scent
And through the night
Turned me to fruit.

I was an apple
Born of a tree.
Through days and nights
Was dreaming so:
For so long I wanted
To hang from a branch.
The rays of the sun
From the heavens – the dew.
How sweet the juice
And red the hue
For whom all this?
Only for you.

But from the tree
You tore me off
Peeled and threw me
Down by your feet.
And all of that, just to have
One bite to eat.

Now see me, oh see
I'm naked and void.
I'm blackened and free
For everyone's mouth.
This apple in here
Which you cracked and peeled
And abandoned, is me.

The bee Escapes

The bee escapes
To the colorful blossom
On your dress:
It will suck from it a
Drink of honey.
I, who hold your picture
Now before me, am much better off,
I suck from it
remembrance.

In Life, all had Passed me By

In life, all had passed me by,
But none of it has disappeared.
Away went all the wars,
But the wounds, I carry still.

And every evening, every evening,
In my heart rise the yearnings,
They tear me and they scatter me
In thousand splinters of remembering.

Dust

Dust

In every land in which I've lived
All that I possessed was that,
Which stuck on to my shoes.

Turning back from every road
With yet another dream despoiled:
I still don't know the taste of land
Only that of dust.

A Small Shtetl

I walk into the market
Congested with anxiety and Jews.
At once I'm being surrounded,
Around me there's a clamor and a row.

They yoke the horse, prepare to leave
On the carts, their paltry things.
But where does one escape? And in which province
Can a Jew now really sleep in peace?

They would like me to opine
And might I have some good advice.
But here comes a Jewish woman,
A blue shawl around her shoulders.

She makes a free path through the street
And with the group of Jews she pleads:
Leave alone that young man, can't you tell,
He's barely standing on his feet?!

She tears me off that gloomy ring
And drags me through the crooked streets.
I sit there on her porch, and in a cup,
She serves me some red borscht.

I sip the borscht — she's overjoyed.
She sips that borscht with me, and I,
I didn't know how rich I was, and wonder
How in every Jewish town — I have a mother.

Armavir *

Armavir!
Do know, it's true:
Another wind
Has come to you.
It is a strange one
That its home it had
Abandoned.
It wanders now
Through vineyards of
Watermelons, apricots.
Drunkenly it sways
Of wine and prairie.
O take it in
And conquer it!

Armavir!
Opened to the prairie are
Your door and gate
I chase and stumble
And I fall exhausted,
Powerless.
But your winds
They are your rulers
Sparing none.

They tear cargoes
They whip rivers
With red hearts
And in the veins
Of young girls
They ferment
The blood!

---

*A town in the Caucasus

Armavir!
From every house
I smell the wine.
Is the wind for you so little
That you wish to be
More drunk?
For, it seems to me:
In every cask and barrel
Lie uncorked
No trickling wine
But your tainted, hot
And restless wind!

Kavkaz *

A. The Sun

At dawn, a wind from all corners, had
Gathered and smitten together the clouds;
They lowered, but the heavens weren't enough
So they also wanted to cover the ground.

It seems that to chase them away
Would be hard, even for seven suns.
Not even the most torrid prayer
From the earth below, would make them depart,

But all of a sudden — the clouds are bright,
The rays spearing, prodding through cracks
They are much wider and the sky is high.

The clouds and the shadows disperse;
The sun that in the heavens reigns
Is now set to conquer the earth.

---

* The Caucasus

B. The Dog

The dog plays peacefully in place
Plays with a ray of light, plays with its tail.
Shakes its paw, and lazily reclines
Like a kitten it tenderly whines

But suddenly it barks with rage
Its eyes, light up with flames
Its teeth sharper, and longer the claws
It's no more a dog, but a wolf.

It falls on the chickens, raid and murder!
The fear which made some chickens fly
Made others – sprint and gallop.

The dog is mad. The dog had bitten a
Hen, and severed its neck,
And it's running around with no head.

C. The Girls

The sky's still hanging like a greasy pan.
The girls are tired of the sluggishness and heat
But just like in a dream: it strikes their tongues,
Their hands, and their feet.

They're like a lovely fairy tale
Somewhere in a children's book,
Lulled to sleep by magic spells
And none of them awoke.

But as the sun sets in the west
It is rekindled in their blood —
It soars and burns in every breast!

It strikes those barely aged sixteen
In the foliage, whispers,
Groans and kisses ... and
Like kindling, lights the trees!

D. The Hawk

After harvest, sack and barn are full.
Now the bird and insect want what's theirs:
This little sparrow, thinking only here
To pluck a seed for a moment's joy.
Only the ants do think ahead:
To provide for tougher days.

The hens were let go from the yard.
And young Tanya, from the kolkhoz.
They carry grain across the prairie.
She sings a song and braids her hair.
Hens look for seeds after the harvest,
And I – for the source of her sweet song.

But what is swiftly cruising high?
The hens do sense the danger, and
Some run in fear, some disappear!
Suddenly the girl is silent.
Her head is up, her face is pale:
– A hawk is hovering! A hawk up high!

The girl who sang so wantonly
How fearfully she cries,
What is she driving at? She winks at me.
Now, I know and understand.
I cry out too, and cry again.
And wonder to myself: how strong I cry!

How strong I cry; bizarre and strange.
My own voice – I do not comprehend.

Not from the throat this cry did come.
It is a pain, a wail, a howl, a roar!
From my bowels from my bones and blood.
They have long waited for that chance!

The hawk descends with talons stretched
To sink into its prey – but
Is scared and swiftly flies away.
The hens, they gather back
And every hen, in the kernel that she picked –
Finds her life restored.

This girl presses my hand with both of hers:
I've helped her with my screams.
The hawk deterred now from the kill.
But soon she is again — standing at her place
Among the hens and starts again
Her sweet and lovely song to sing.

This girl, she sings, but I — I cry.
When the hawk assailed my home,
Into my closest, talons plunged —
I did not shield them, I was far
And rescued but myself.
This girl, she sings, but I – I cry.

A Strange Spring

A garden like a fairytale:
On the trees pink blooms
My teeth want soon to bite
The round – ripe apricots.
Like honey in my mouth
Letting out sweet juice.

The grapevine wrapped with leaves
Over windows, walls and gates
With luck will later hang
Large bunches of grapes.
I can already taste the wine,
I will sing its praise.

But when I see the cherry trees
Blooming in white wonder
My distant home returns
Woe is me! I shudder,
The apricots – are bitter.
And the sweet wine is sour.

The way Back

A sandy desert here, as far as one can see!
Something here is touching and reminding me.
And something is aflame
Still farther from the farthest is in me
My childhood —
The childhood of grandfathers.
Should I look for traces?
Should I ask for proof?
Wasn't childhood cradled
On the humps of camels?
Can't someone find a trace
On me, when I do speak,
And on my face?

Oh, east!
Receive a son
A long – lost one.
So what if I was born
In another land?
I have not sucked the juice
Of those far away green fields.
But just the milk
Of mother dear, dear breast.
My home is empty there
Amidst the ruins.
Shirtless, barefoot, only
With the word of justice
Burning in my mouth,
I come now as I did
A long, long time ago.

Tashkent 1941

Bridal Veil

The girls remain, so, in my thoughts:
A bright smile on a darker cheek
The sun had baked them succulent...
And a little smoky from above.

But outside their house, the faces
Now are covered with thick veils
And people say these women
Are — old and obsolete.

It would thus need to always be:
Beauty, when its luster fades and withers
In late autumn of the years —

It should be veiled. It should not rudely
Of old age, be weakened and ashamed,
But in the glory of our thoughts remain.

Women Waiting

The women are waiting for bread,
And meanwhile lead a conversation;
Calmly joins them — Mister Death,
And waits with them in procession.

One woman talks of her son,
The other – of her husband;
They are very far from the front,
And also, with them they are present.

Death overhears the chat:
— My husband is far with the army;
I stand by the window, distressed,
And await a word or a letter.

But when a letter is brought,
In me, wells up the fear;
Is he from the hospital writing?
I dread to open the door ...

The second: should my son return
With no leg, or no eyes... oh
Just let him come home —
He'll still be my child.

The third one heartily says:
— The war rages on and on.
The days are hard for the men,
But hard for the wives are the nights ...

As each of them now is musing,
The line quickly transforms:
Death has turned up quite a bit,
And all see it now for themselves!

They look at death, all in shock –
With disgust, with woe and fear.
Till they hear the vendor's shout:
— Bread! At last the bread is here.

A flame lights up in each eye,
The place is tearing apart:
One woman becomes a dog,
A second – enraged like a cat.

With nails or indeed with their teeth,
Bread they all must get!
In the corner stands all by himself
Insulted, and shamed, Mister Death...

Ballad of the Poplar Tree

In Tashkent City, in Navoy Street,
There grows and blooms a poplar tree.

From early morning the sun,
Is lustily burning its crown.

But — content with dreaming, it sleeps
All stars are lovely, but it loves just one.

And comes the night, the poplar wakes,
And to a star extends its plea:

— You golden star, above my crown,
I long for you, please come and shine.

I'm here below, denuded of leaves.
I'm here below – so dusty and beat.

I stand exposed, and come what may:
The warmth or indeed, the saw and ax,

But I don't care, believe me it's true,
For over all, I raise my head, to you.

And may even the blue jay sing
Of earthly joys – and cheer.

I am not taken by his magical song.
And painfully to him it whispers still:

How slowly I grow! I would like
To have been a plume of smoke —

Reaching up to the sky, quickly, upward,
Even though in there, might come my demise.

And in the clouds my life be lost —
Let it be, as long as to you I'm close!

And days go by, and day after day
A hot sun burns, in the city of Tashkent.

But night after night also there shines
The magic stars in the dark-blue sky,

And it's hard for the sun to understand, those
Who in the morning long for the stars.

Till once in a day of the month of May,
When people are out walking free

In white clothes, white shoes and hats,
The trees erupt with blossoms white.

The people and trees, are all in white,
But now a dark speck, a growing cloud.

And soon the whole sky
Is dressed in black.

The whole sky – black, the earth is white
And all at once – a storm blares out!

From the wastelands, bursting forth.
How wild it howls, how raging and loud!

From the desert returned,
To take everything, to the desert back.

The head unkempt the body sways
Eagerly the poplar cries and wails:

— A storm! I have dreamed of the day, when
I'd be taken, and carried, away to the stars!

The storm now meanly roars at him
A veil descends and spins him 'round.

Branches spread like wings of a bird,
Ready to fly.

Up to the stars, it longs to fly
And on the ground, dead it falls!

And with the stars, what's further true —
The stars are lovely but people are fooled —

For, they are cold, and if a tree should fall, then
What of that? A new forest soon will grow.

Dreaming poplars have their heights,
But I must toil for every rhyme.

The Foot-Steps Song

Until with striding I acquainted once became,
Father used to hold me by my right hand,
And mother by the left. In the middle
I would set out with a feeble gait.
Then, all by myself I tried this path:
Hold the table, closet and the bed
Fall and rise, and start again.
Until I picked myself, up from the dust,
Until I'd placed each of my steps
Like a seal upon the earth: I had arrived.

I firmly stepped upon the earth,
For I resolved: where I had walked,
There, was my home and place. But, oh
The ground beneath my feet caught fire,
And like dynamite, tore from under me
All that my soles had touched.

I then set out upon the road
Walking days and nights.
In children's stories heroes quickly move
But, where are your magic shoes
When every road is spanning seven miles?
No one had gifted me such shoes.

And then I felt by walking so:
The bumpiness of every rock
The heat from the asphalt,
The dampness of the woods.

The dust of the dirt road
And the frost of night.
The globe became earmarked by soil
Just like a map upon my soles.

While someone is so destined
To measure with a wheel the size of earth
The sky – with wings, the ocean —
With a steamer or a sail,
I — I've been condemned and must
This whole life move by foot.
Pay for all the things that life would give —
With walking, till the final step.

I know not, of any debt.
For every scaling to the mountain-top
For every distance — every time
With foot-steps, with their own reward.
And, until my sun will set,
I will keep walking just like that
And on my going back, no steps I'll take,

And all good people with me I shall take.

Smoke

Smoke

A

This wasn't smoke from a hut in the village, quiet and measured,
the mild wind carrying it from the chimney to heaven,
incorporating it into itself: a blue cloud.

B

It was not the smoke from a city factory, thick and fat,
rising up and dispersing, but leaving riches down below,
fabric, machines and furniture.

C

And this was not the smoke of an orchard in the fall: sated,
languid, smoke of fallen leaves that the gardener collected in a
pile and burned, so that the trees might give their fruit with
abundance.

D.

But it was the smoke from the chimneys of the crematoria
fiery and bloody – of my mother, my sister and brothers.
The smoke, which I always see, rise from every factory and hut
and pile of leaves in autumn gardens.

I Come Home

The house would likely be the same,
I will unlock the gate:
Neighbors will come up to greet me,
But in there, I will not find my kin.

The old furniture will be there too,
Though the people — will be new.
Strangers sleep in our beds,
And at the table strangers eat their bread.

At the window there will stand
A flower-pot.
And on the wall quietly hanging
A still and hallowed icon.

And in the corner, there's a crib
And in the crib – a blue eyed child;
To the child, from a green cage,
Sweetly sings a bird.

In that room, don't they hear the silent
Rustling and the murmuring of shadows?
In that room, don't they feel
The cold breath of the crying graves?

After sausage, cabbage and some schnapps,
They slumber peacefully as one.
But won't the child wake up
From his dream and cry?

If not even the child will wake,
The bird will turn to a raven
And call for death and ruin,
Of both the child and icon!

A Bombed House

They loved to decorate the rooms:
Various colors on the walls, and
On the walls still hanging from above
The pictures of their kin and of themselves.
The porches overgrown with vines, untamed.
Upon the window sills are flower pots
Over them the small white curtain covers
Keeping private things from foreign eyes.

And if a hoary piece of furniture
Did break, it seemed, it's part of life:
So many ways to memories it bonds!
All prepared in here, for months and years:
In here, all summer long, the women cooked.
In the cupboard, jars and bottles stood
With cherries wild and gooseberry wine
For treating guests in better times.

Here they dreamed and yearned, here a woman
Was with child, and wondered in her heart:
Whose eyes the child will get,
Her blue eyes, or the father's — cherry black.
And it was a house without a hope. From here
The children sailed across wide oceans
To hot lands, to see giants and dwarves.
In every place life left its mark.

The doors were there like mouths, so large
Each one wanted from without, to bring in
All it could. In there, an old man

Was delirious, and for the first time dreamed:
Here, a miracle will happen... just
This time ... and he will live and never die ...
But death rose higher and rose higher still,
And life itself is hiding now in pits.

Fearfully the people hear the thunder:
God does fling his lightning onto trees and men
And when dark clouds would gather, men
Soon tremble, stammering a prayer
Till at the end arrived a savior
Who restrained the cruelty of gods.
But who protects a man from murder,
And who will give him and his child a home?

This house did not escape the tempest.
A bomb had dropped destroying all
That sat there for so many years,
And all that was secured under a lock
And dotted on, pampered and caressed
Became at once ruined and lost!
The wanton wind, unhindered, breaking doors
Rioting, carousing in most private lots.

Many years had passed silent and idle,
Till suddenly the bricks – they stirred
Tore from the walls, a chase, a fling:
Barely can the people, shun their fate
And can't protect the house from danger –

Leave you buried here, let you here be covered
Until the ones we trust will come: the children
Women and ourselves will build again.
And of the great house which is now destroyed
A half-denuded wall, is still upright
And on the wall (what a surprise!) a cage:
On a branch, there hops a bird like mad
And sings a little, and argues and laments,
Here I can no longer stay, I must get off,
Because the thought takes hold of me:
I am myself the bird,
The bird lamenting in the ruins.

In a Dream

No more corpses now at school
As if your childhood is made-up
The schools in here, are all destroyed
Seek them just in dreams at night.

My dream is all of a dead world
It comes to me as far as this:
Father, mother, brothers, friends,
relatives… and neighbors.

I live like I once did, in the same
House. We sit and have some food
I speak, I'm counseled, I confide,
Such ordinary, daily stuff.

But breaks the dawn, and I feel sick,
I wake with terror and with sweat:
How painful is it: through the nights
I live in a world of the dead.

So, no longer seek the dead at school,
The schools already are destroyed,
And in the cemetery look for them no more –
You'll only find them in your dreams.

Crying

On Fridays mother used to bless the lights
Her hands were covering her face
And praying — to the lights she turned.
Then, she would lower down her hands –
A little longer, staying stiff,
Her face flushing, red with tears.

I was amazed and asked myself:
How do to mother, quickly come
Tears to her eyes each time?
Though she cries much, she still has more.
I sometimes, too, wanted to cry:
When in the hospital there was great wailing
By the dead, or when I wanted from mother
To obtain a toy, or a fresh fruit.
But as much as I had squeezed and rubbed my eyes,
The brightness stayed in them intact.
Once, a trick I fabricated, and my eyes I wetted
But people knew and laughed,
Because of that, now I am pretty good:
I close my eyes for just a trice
And think of my old home:
Not only can I shed a pallid tear,
But bleed a river, bring a flood!

And, my every word — is backed with blood.

Wild Vine

Once there was a house,
That each and every morning
Opened up itself to life
With toil.
And each evening
Closed up inside itself
Over the night –
The love.

Down came a bomb
Upon the house
And it's again just
Bricks.
Dumb.
No more.

The wild vine ruggedly contends:
If there won't be
More life in there
It would grow inside
Like — up to here.

On walls it quakes
And so it says:
Around all blooms
The sky is blue.
I grow and rise
Up and up.
And you just hush -
Live on, wake up!

But still, this house is dead.
Burned.
Annihilated
Gone.

How sad are now
The living leaves
Upon dead walls.

Shalom Aleichem*   (Peace upon you)

When on Fridays, my brother
Used to go back home from school
His heart reposed and filled with song
And a table for him waited
With Challah* bread,
With meat and fish, and too,
Accompanied him loyally:
Angels three.

But when my brother in a
Frosty, windy
Winter's day,
Was ordered to undress,
And with shouts and dogs
Behind
Chased to the gas –
Where were then
His three angels?

Only one angel
Did appear —
The angel of death.
Not as he's known
By the people for so long:
A skeleton devoid of flesh and skin
With scythe in hand,

But firm and slim.
With blonde hair and blue eyes
Of a savage forest pedigree
And poison blowing from his mouth.

As my brother saw him,
He spread his hands apart,

Pressed his teeth
And averted
His pale face.
And did not wish,
No, he did not wish,
To say to him,
Shalom aleichem.

---

* The conventional spelling of 'ch' in Aleichem and Challah, is pronounced
like 'kh'

A Moment of Silence

For the memory of the holy departed
We shall be for a moment silent.
In that silence I can hear, the rushing
And the seething of their blood.

I feel a cold wind crying
And hear their silent steps.
Oh see, oh see: the dead are
Walking in our midst.

They're coming now from all the roads
Their numbers very large.
In this moment I die
Six million times.

And they – they live again
Again, six million times.
My sisters and my brothers
From the deep valley of the bones.

They rise at the front and the back,
At the left and at the right,
Trapped we had become
In the dark ring of demise.

The circle gets more crowded,
We cannot, no we cannot escape
Who is just a shadow,
And who does really live?

The dead are no more shadows,
Tortured and gassed, they breathe
With the same air that
We now hold inside.

They search, and look at each
And every single face,
One found, what a wonder –
A relative, one found a friend.

Most don't find a soul in here
None of their kin,
They are mourned, and
Remembered with a tear.

Let us all remember them,
Their holy blood demands revenge,
Their holy blood demands revenge!

A Letter

You, who are my childhood friend
You, who've known me for so long,
Oh come to me, oh come drive up,
Because I am now, sick at heart ...

Because you are the last, the only
One; from then until today.
No one believes of what I speak
No one believes this thing I say.

Oh come through land and sea,
And testify to large and small
That I too, had a mother
And didn't grow out of a stone ...

That that's the crib wherein I lay
Where brothers five had rocked me.
And that the parents used to
Call me their 'sixth joy' ...

That my home, a fortress was
With a porch under the roof...
I used to check against its walls,
How much I grew the previous night...

That I had played with, and grew up
With animals and house pets,
The dog, the cat, the goat and bird,
The family was big, God-bless.

All yielding in the moment
All standing in its place
In the evenings, for the sake of
Catching crickets the cat left.

The moon did not appeal to me
(Its face was green and jaundiced)
The dog opposing it would stand
Until the morning, howling, yowling …

A bully used to bother me —
The goat rammed him with its horns
The bird knew what I said in Yiddish,
And answered me right back: you dolt…

And, bear witness that my eyes
Now grey – once, they were blue,
And the wrinkles now I have,
Weren't always drawn across my face.

As I played with a child of a friend
He looked me in the eye and asked
A prickly question, just like that:
— Were you once, like me, a child?

I did not answer, I was dumb
Because suddenly I felt
That saying "yes" would be a lie —
And so I said: good night!

Leave your home and start your trip,
Come now my friend, come quick!
And be my witness, so the world may know
And above all — my good friend's child.

Elegy to Yiddish

Yak Yiddish — To doydish, (From a folk-song)

My mother taught me how to speak,
When I was very small and weak
Since then, I've spoken to them all,
But none would comprehend my tongue.
T'was too uproarious and simplistish
She had taught me to speak Yiddish.

Even a cock, at dawn delighting,
Gets a replying crow, much to his liking.
A dog makes too, a joyous face
At night, when it's responding — to a yelp
How can it be, then, for anyone a novelty
When I want to hear my Yiddish spoken fluently?

And so when comes to me a phrase
I smell it, taste it, try it for some time.
But if I lack a proper one,
As long as I don't find it – I'm undone.
Poetically refined and not simplistish,
I would defend all words in Yiddish.

And oftentimes it seems, the fathers and
The mothers, who were killed by
German hands still live with us,
They died with their first language.
Therefore, don't say a Kadish* but make Kiddush*
When you open up a book of Yiddish.
Will Yiddish live much longer? This – people
Would debate, but I – I swear:
Yiddish will exist as long as in my veins
Will seethe my mother's tear
Till you, my soul, rest in your die-dish
And this, will be my final rhyme in Yiddish.

---

* Therefore: do not bless the Lord, but make a sacrament

From: **Last Writings**

By the Rivers of Babylon...

By the rivers of Babylon
They sat,
And the old homes
Could not forget.

On the willows of Babylon
Fiddles are hanging:
But in a foreign land
Hard is the singing.

But I, the grandchild
Blasphemous — disgraced,
Already called my home
Who knows how many lands?

Wasn't home the land
Where my cradle stood?
Where I, the first time stammered
Ma... mama... mother?

Wasn't home the land
Where feverish I was
Where I first heard:
'Darling' and 'beloved'?

And when I was a child
Wasn't mother singing
When up a tree I was
Merrily swinging?

And from the flowing rivers
Water sweet I drank,
How with simple joy
In them I dove and swam.

When from my eyes was gone
That distant home of mine —
I still could hear the rushing
Of local trees and streams.

But no, enough for now
Song of mine, be still!
Let calm rush in
And rock no more.

Once again, start over?
No! I can no longer,
Like the grandfathers from a willow,
I will hang you up, my song.

Of all the homes I had,
This one is the meanest,
For wherever there's a willow
Someone there is weeping.

Going Back…

Oh, a child's reminiscence!
I used to, sometimes read a book,
And with curiosity and strain,
Search in the story, for the end.

I would mix up the times,
Gazing forward, skipping 'cross the lines
Blessed childhood times!
Now, I wish to skip right back…

Wife and Child

On the great seas, sails a ship
Swiftly cruising to this place,
And carries here and bringing me
My wife and child.

You, wild storm, now be serene
Do become a zephyr wind.
Rave not madly — lull to sleep
My wife and child.

Resounding thunder — now be mute!
You angry lightning — disappear!
Do not scare, nor wake from sleep
My wife and child.

Captain! Grip the helm — securely in your hands
Don't plow sightless through the sea
For there is no one left for me,
Except my wife and child.

Oh God! I know that I am weak
And moreover full of sin
But do not punish for my deeds
A mother and a child.

A white seagull flies and flies
Still faster than the wind;
There – stand upon the deck
My wife and child.

And looking silently, amazed,
And greets them kindly now
The seagull is my song
To wife and child.

If the Child Will Ask

Oh, woman! We shall yet
Have a child,
And our child will utter
The first words of love:
Mama and papa.

But also may yet come a time:
This child, when seeing a grandfather
That sits his friend upon his knee,
And sings to him, and tells him tales
Of voyages, wizards and dwarves,
Will wonder, and of both of us
Inquire: where is my grandpa?
What answer is for his complaint?
It will choke me in my throat.
(My father died so long ago,
and yours was killed by German hands)

And if he played with the neighbor's child
There he will see – a bespectacled grandmother,
Knitting socks or a sweater,
To keep her grandchild warm in the cold weather
Will our child now ask,
Where is my uncle where's my aunt?
Will we then know, or be allowed
To tell him of the pain and horror?
(And that my mother, and then yours,
The German murderers, buried alive?)

And the friend of our child
Having uncles, having aunts,
To his birthday, they would come
Each one, bringing a present:

Dominos, bicycle or a ball.
Will our child come home, and ask:
Where are my uncles and my aunts?
And we'll be startled, pale and numb.
(For my siblings, and yours too,
The German murderers killed!)
And if the child's friend will one day
Get married — as fine people do:
There will come, from near and far
His aunts and uncles, for he isn't just
His parent's child,
But the son of all of them as one.
But to his wedding, our son will be escorted
By no one, besides us two — no one else at all
And all the fiddles, basses, flutes —
Will they lament and cry?

Like a Truth

At times you do not please me, but I tell you: you are lovely
(For tomorrow you can light up with another charm.)

And though odds favor it be wrong, I tell you: it is true
(For tomorrow acting well, you indeed, can cheer me up.)

For what I say in love is same as what I write:
It is imagined — and just the same, like a truth survives.

Spring

From every street and roof
The snow's already gone.
A woman takes a look,
At the mirror on the wall,
And clearly sees with dread:

On her black hair, now it seems
Some snow remained.

She opens up the closet
Looking for a dress.
She has been picking long
Puts on a dress and sees:
— It clearly is too big.
A second — and she spots:
It is on her too loose.
A third — and she now says:
— Ah God, how do I look!

And quietly and sadly,
That dress — she's taking off.

As such as does a tree
With its leaves in fall,
And prepares for winter time.

This Poem was also featured in 'Woe and wander' under the title
'A Jewish woman'

A Visitor

It's late at night
I hear a knocking on the door.
I open it
And before me stands a rendition —
A strange apparition.

— Who are you? — I ask.
— I'm an old song of yours.

And I am amazed: could I as well be told,
How and when?

— All by yourself you can, you can…

I look and answer: no.
He replies as though he cries:
— The mother, brothers, sister,
Wafting with the smoke.

Did you forget them
Even for a minute?
I've been like them, indeed
Your own flesh and blood.

Recall the days of war
You had created me
And soon forgotten me
On a distant wandering road;
Since then I had no rest.

And what I'm now,
Here, see, acquaint yourself:
He removes his coat
And all that tears away
Is wind.

When you abandoned me
I turned to air,
I wandered over land
Looking for a body
In a beast, a tree, or stone —
And couldn't find it, for I was
Destined to be,
Nothing but a song.
I had to meet you
Like a Jew yearning for God
And a song, yearning to be born.

… A whole night I lay awake
Kissed, caressed, rejoiced
And did not separate
From my retrieved lost song.

A Winter's Night

In the street the rain is pouring
And possibly the snow.
You put up the teapot
To brew for us some tea.

How cold now in the room,
How dim the light does burn
Oh, dear! Take now the coat,
Quickly off your back.

I kiss your fingers, and
I tell you: it is here,
A song I just did write.
For whom — I won't divulge.

(The cold water is freezing
The teapot's inner parts,
But from the soaring flame
It is now warming up.)

How warm it has become
How warm and also bright
We have the coats already
Quickly taken off.

(The teapot now is warm
Listen how it soon
Be whispering and hissing
A quiet lovely tune.)

We have forgotten all,
Whatever happens — let it roll!
The night is drawing longer
Like in the northern pole.

(The teapot's lid is rising
It sprinkles, boils and seethes
The water's almost gone
It soon will burst from heat.)

—What is it with the teapot?
— It faithfully boiled out…
Both of us, embarrassed,
Again, we fill it up.

Heaven and Earth

People always fight for land,
And by a mountain, field or house,
They all want to hang their banners,
They want to put their border posts.

Pity the children at school,
That study during such times,
They get acquainted with the world
And people change the maps.

But the heavens stay the same.
They are too high and far
Still as blue as Genesis, the
Smoke can't make it dark.

If the stars were standing near
Then kings would have them stitched
To their clothes like buttons, and
Nail them to their shoes.

And if a nimble hunter
Shot a constellation,
The Milky-Way would be now trampled,
And flowing with star-blood

But from heaven the sun still pours its gold
And in the night the moon rains silver
And in heaven – there are
No border-posts and banners.

First Light

I awoke. The darkness
Attacked my hands and feet.
It had already gulped
All things inside the room,
Now it will take me
With its last crunch.

This is not a room
But an inkwell prison –
I am a fly
And when I try
To move a wing, there is
A wall, and I fall back.

I look for the electric
Switch, I look for it
With eagerness, blindly
Like a child, searching
With his mouth, for his
Mother's breast.

And suddenly — a wonder:
Light! A dot is bursting
On the ceiling, and
All things have sucked from it
Their color and their form.

The wall is whiter now.
The mirror shimmers, bright;
The chair receives four legs,
Now it is up on two,
And promptly starts to dance.

And I — with white bed sheets
I cover — wrap myself,
Away from a dark wave,
Surging from a coast
Of calm and loveliness.

You Wait

You wait — for the future
Frightened of the crow
The crow is really black
But the day is bright.

Do you wait forever?
The hour now is hacked
The earth — it isn't black.

You wait like this and wait
For that, which isn't there,
When so much black in you
Is longing to be bright.

All that for which you wait,
Is waiting here for you.
At heart it's never dark
When eyes are looking blue.

Additional Poems

Ballade of the Three Hanged Partisans

A. The bee

A bee flies through, flies buzzing by
But seven fold as hard as flying —
Is the sadness of her song.
O, golden bee do tell, disclose,
The reason for your sadness now,
I want to hear, I want to know.

I flew to see an apple tree,
To gather nectar from its blooms,
But suddenly I stopped in shock—
O, bleak oppressive tale it was!

What I saw I couldn't bear!
I fear the honey's gone from me
And I can only poison give.
The stream of honey in me dried
O, come with me, down there to see.

B. The tree

Here is the tree, and here I see:
Nefarious hand of German crime
Had changed the tree to gallows;
Three partisans with honor dead
Three blood-red stars, cut in their breasts.

O, apple tree in bloom, in white
How did you change into a gallows
From a happy children's tale?

You, who must have heard the crying —
Great men choking wheezing, dying —
How will you bloom in white again?

How will you pour into your apples
Nectar sweet and summer wine
And paint their cheeks in sunny reds?
And in the moment of their deaths
Did you at least desire —
To wilt and die along with them?

C. The storm

Could the tree no more be hushed
Hastily lower its limbs
Waking up the hanging men?
Hear them whisper to each other
See their hanging bodies swing —
Swaying like the tongues of bells.

Now a whirlwind starts on land
Rivers rushing, flowing fast
Beasts now bellow like they're hunted
And the whirlwind turns to storm.

Climb upon the highest towers
Tear down all the flags and banners,
Here the storm soars in the gardens
Plucks the blossoms as they bloom
No more fruit now for your foes.

Here the storm leaps to the blacksmith,
Smacks the forge and carries sparks
Sets ablaze the enemies' barn.

D. Portent

Hear a whisper, hear a voice:
Winds are howling it's a warning
That injustice happened here,
And will happen yet again;
Enemy soldiers standing pale
Winds are howling a worse portent —
And looking for a resting place.

But should they look for forest shelter —
Partisans in arms await:
Behind the trees, behind the shrubs;
And should they seek a mountain shelter,
Partisans will swarm from caves
Hurl them down into the voids.
Who could calm the rushing storm?
In the place of three — a thousand
From town and village, cellar, shack.
Blessed are their deeds and suffering!
Down the streets, in place of gallows
A monument will ever live!

Tashkent July 10, 1942

I Invite you to a Masquerade-Ball

1

For all of those asphyxiated
In the previous war by gas
Or burned; for all who will by gas
Asphyxiated be in the next war
This is an admonition. I,
Invite you to a masquerade-ball.
Prepare for it, prepare; it will
Be quite superb, original,
And will include both old and young
And not just people, not just men,
A horse in stable, even dogs,
And all the guests will wear a mask.
The dance is odd, exotic, strange:
They turn and fling themselves, and they
Don't hear, how bizarre the music is,
That none can follow it,
Not even if they froze.

2

Bells are ringing, sirens too,
Though the appointed time
Is yet unknown and could be far,
Or could be at the crack of dawn.
The ticket price is low: for admission
Each and every one should pay
No more than his budding life;
Thus the professor states; he's touched,
In suit and tails, all black
Such joy is bubbling from the heart
Makes worthwhile all the weariness

And all his florid gab.
Such gas as he concocted
Until today no one has found,
It smothers, poisons and destroys
People animals and stuff.
Not for nothing all reporters
Are attending — not for nothing
The defenders of the fatherland
Their welcome now extend.

3

Proudly will your name be uttered,
How beautiful it is declaimed,
How sweet. The professor, now, is truly
Moved, caressing now his wife
And says like so — I thank my wife
Who loves the smell of flowers, but
For myself, I love the more
Genteel smell of perfume, thank
Their fine and magic formulation.
We do not love the objects but
Their scent. I'm thankful that the Lord,
On the altar never eats
His victims' flesh, but just inhales
Their smoke, ha, ha.
Not a prophet or a fool,
Not a comet in the sky,
Have announced this danger, but
From newspapers have risen little
Snake-heads spinning webs of hate.

4

And false telegrams and rumors,
That just the neighbor is to blame

Just he alone, and still, and yet
Of his spilled blood our hands are clean.
Writers soon dream up the heroes
Officers conceive of medals
And promotions. Ministers —
Assume their own historic place.
Bankers dream of digging gold
And oil-wells, manufacturers —
Dream of praise — a spot for all
But came the day when madness grabbed
The reins of all the senses, and,
That flared and burned with lies and hate.
No Salamander issued it,
But such an animal for which
Zoology does not have names
And which is simply known as war!

5

Many years in labs they toiled
Mixing chemicals;
Generals kept it secret, but
Now it is revealed.
This web of lunacy and hatred:
Gas!!!
First letters from the front, and
Cities seized by fear,
Naively setting up their shields.
People are afraid
To pick fruit from a branch
Water from the spring
To tread water, take a step,
Maybe it is tainted,
Ruined from the operation!!!
A bird flies over a wall — an airplane!!!
A bee is buzzing by — an airplane!!!

A burning mouth — is suspect! Gas!
People grab their children, screaming, gas!
Like a mole would dig itself
Into the ground.

6

Of nothing wished to be acknowledged,
Nothing is perceived,
But lying down, informed, but still
Misguided following each other,
Thinking of some better times,
Guarding… self-deluded
And suddenly church-bells are ringing
Trains are screeching, sirens weeping
Alarms blaring, the air is shaken
With screaming and ringing — airplanes!!!
Terror descends on everyone
Animals restless around the stables
Dogs bite themselves out of their chains!
They howl and bark.
Children can't be pacified.
Women fall convulsing, people
Seal all windows, close all doors
They close the curtains but
Are restless still.

7

Death can sneak in, through a lock
And the airplanes are approaching.
On the train-station drops a bomb
In the air fly wood and brick and stone
Wagons crash into a pile of chips
What was here before, no one can tell
And the planes are coming, closer still,

There drops a bomb with death and fire
Across the street they run, they cry, they scream.
But soon they halt they cough, asphyxiate
From mouth and nose the blood is coming, thumping
They fall and burble out a word of
Horror, curse and hate!!!
Gas!!!
From a house runs out a pregnant woman
Her lips are blue, her face is pale.

8

She wants to cross the street
She is in pain
Pained through all her limbs
A cry!!! She falls.
Blood is showing — flowing,
A rivulet below the tramway rails
A child is born right in the street and
His first breath is drawing gas!!!
Rejoice world rulers now,
Your gas worked out!

Over my Head in the Canopy

Over my head in the canopy
A bird sings a cheerful song,
And doesn't even know that I
Am hiding in the dark below,
And that I hate the sun
That in the clearing brings me death.

Oh leaves I know: it's autumn now
I miss the decomposing earth,
Oh leaves, oh please, do not fall down!
A friend is dying and I will
In yellow foliage hide my head.

In his fever my friend spoke
And I am thunderstruck with fright,
The wind abruptly fanned the flames
Of all the burning homes. And
Over the mountains and the valleys
Cries my friend, the wounded hero:
For everything — we shall pay back!

By the road the huts are burning
The black night mirrored in red flames.
The black night envies them and can't,
No it cannot, recognize itself.

It would have liked to be ablaze
Eviscerate the body, kill the joy
Of gray old men and children —
Those who once, to sleep were rocked
With a lovely tale of the little white goat.

Still follows me the old Jew of Kaluszyn:
Don't forsake me, where are you going, where?

War*

In the darkness — blind the houses stand
(Light must not be seen by the enemy's planes)
But the heavens not being afraid,
Into the night, set the stars ablaze.

The dreaming women see their men fall
By their destroyers – crying in their sleep,
But calm and peacefully do sleep the sheep,
And in the stalls the horses and the beasts.

A peasant travels on a wagon by
To the front, accompanies his son,
His pain and sorrow he has drowned in wine.

At the well a pail hangs on a rod.
And from the well — no longer water brings
It is drunk of moonlight now.

---

* This poem also appeared in 'Woe and wander' under the title 'Night'

Little Hens

First hen:
Hens! with wings, do make a flail –
Tell the world it is now day.

Hens:
It's really day? it really is?
How do you know, oh say, oh say!

First hen:
A smart hen doesn't really ask,
But feels it straight and blurts it out.

Second hen:
(Recites)
It is for me as clear as day
For me and them; it's not
The hen that brings the day
But the day — that brings the cluck.

First hen:
Oy vey and woe to such a hen
Who, at dawn sits idle still!

Third hen:
I wait here for a sign that shows,
That it is really, truly, dawn.

First hen:
Soon, the light, in windows shines
And in the workshops men will come.

Third hen:
Does not a whole night burn away
While it's the sick who are awake?

First hen:
One doesn't see the stars up high —
For it's the sun that blinds the eye.

Fourth hen:
I think, one cannot see the stars
Because the clouds are in the sky.

Hens:
Till break of day till it will shine
One should, one must alert the crowd.

(Dawn comes, the sun goes higher and higher)

Hens:
Can one though possibly... just ask?
It seems, one can, one may... one must...
Now it is safe, there is no harm.

(The hens courageously flail their wings and crow furiously)

Wake up you lazy from your sleep!...

Moral:
I do not like hens that crow by day when the sun
is already up in the sky.

The Great Thieves (A fable)

Mice, as you must know, are nothing but a plague;
They gnaw and nibble night and day.
Had someone placed a cage inside the house
And all was locked and sealed,
A mouse could no more nibble 'cause
His young wife isn't brave
She sees a mouse – she's horrified, she faints!

And just as much as she hates mice
She just adores, she loves a cat.
How diligent it is, how clean!
And also loves a warm and comfy spot.
And so the cat slinks silently around
Here a nibble, there a lick —
Of hunger? — God forbid! It's only curious.
The hunger — it is just for mice.

And suddenly it sees a box;
(That it's a cage, it once did hear —
But it forgot — it happens oftentimes to cats)
And in the trap a piece of fat.

So the cat leaps, grabs — a catch!
But faster goes the trap: a drop, a clap!
The cat — it meows, it wails, it cries
(Less from the pain than from surprise)
But soon it gives a pull, a shove —
And stands again on its own paws.

If that did happen to a mouse
Then it would surely stay entrapped,
Its fate would be all sealed and done.
But bigger thieves — they all get out.

The Little White Goat

Who is the little white goat,
That's coming now toward me?
It walked with me from the cradle
In all my roads beside me.

Eating grass out of my hands
And moss from broken roofs
The roofs have all burned down
The hands — are empty now.

Her rugged wool plucked-out
From vermin and from thorns
The burden of this world
Bending down its horns.

The grass from father's roof
That yellow grew, and meager
Here grows so green and plenty
But for a stranger — bitter.

A bird — is small and weak,
However it has wings
The heavens are its roof
It doesn't guard a crib.

It flies above the ground
And if it wishes, higher.
O God, restore our homes
And give the goat a byre.

It is Such a Weather

At evening quietly, the snow came down
And tried to cling onto the ground
But the earth, not for a moment
Would let it stay around.

So again it tried its luck,
On the trees and rooftops:
Here it lies — a coat so thin
And keeps on piling higher still.

The frost now helps the snow
And grabs the earth, and shrinks it
And dries up all the rivers,
And freezes all the swamps.

Uh-oh, the frost is far and wide
The snow is spreading still
I quickly don the fur-coat
And step onto the sleigh!

But when the morning comes
You may not realize
The daring of the frost
Is slowly trickling out.

Uh-oh! It melts and flows
And there is no more snow
The rain had swept it out
Like in the street, the dust.

The rain keeps pouring down,
It seems, the earth below
Is soaking to its core,
Fermenting, waking up.

For a long time did the sun
Dry the bark for naught;
In just one day the earth
Became so very soft,

That the rain can pull a tree
A big one, with its roots
With its left weaker hand,
From the soaking, rotting earth.

Soon, all the houses sink
Up to their chimneys,
And all that's left around
Is clean, loose dirt.

But see: the sun now shining
With thousand colors, and
Treats the wounded earth
With trails of bandages.

I Walked Back From the Well

I walked back from the well
And evening softly spread.
The yoke was on my shoulders
With water in two pails.

The water pails are heavy
So heavy I am straining —
Not like it's water, but as if
I'm carrying my yearning.

And suddenly my love
Grows straight before my eyes
I stand and on my shoulders
The water pails, they jar.

Is she — is she like always,
Still beautiful and fair
We stand and talk, and talk—
The moon is overhead.

Here asking me with wonder
Why are you standing lost
The pails across your shoulders
And breaking now your bones?

I too, carry a burden
And I, as if I felt —
My shoulders not with burden
But a load of nimble air.

The Single Line

I was walking in the street and there I met
A group of men, running as one.
I went between them, and I heard:
— A man fell down from hunger, that is all.

So I came home, and tried to write a song
That should be full of fiery cries
driving in the streets, calling for struggle,
But could not write more than one line:
— A man fell in the street from hunger.

I see a thin, mature and bristly face
I feel I won't forget him that fast.
And hear: if you really want to find your peace
In just one line as mundane as it is,
If not you, if not you — the poor sad singer,
Who will know that a man has fallen from hunger?

So I will write this song and do not know what else.
This line repeats once, and again.
My heart is heavy and I contemplate:
This line repeats once, and again.
Then I exclaim: no, I can no longer go
How can I write when earlier I saw,
In the street, a man falling from hunger.

It's been already days that I don't know
With me what is the matter:
Wherever I find, a piece of paper,
I clutch it and write on it once more:
A man fell in the street from hunger.

The Song of sun and Gold

We stretch our haggard hands to heaven
Every morning with a prayer: the sun.
We drop to earth a clod of dirt
And after work at evening: gold;
Not receiving not attaining what we want.

With what, with what should we unpack,
From the steely wide outgrowing treasury
That gold, and from heaven the hard sun?
Other eyes, extinguished stars, they twinkle not.

Black rings like tears, like shackles pulling 'round
What can they still… still light
If not the sun — that poor man's gold
Or if not gold — sun of the blind.

Our hands, what can they do for us, our hands,
But always wring from deep sharp pain, and
Bruise the fists with frantic rage,
What can they — then, our blind hands do —
Not fortified by gold, not painted by the sun?

Sun and gold, gold and sun, and sun and gold again,
Eternally desired — never meant for us to gain.
And if our poverty remains, then what is left for us
But spitting at the heavens and bloodying the earth.

Poem of the Locked up Gates

Winter-night, the early hour.
Israel Aszendorf goes home
Now from the city.
Snow and whirlwind and locked gates.
But, he goes confronting snow,
Confronting wind, confronting fate.

One gate is locked.
A second, a third, all is constrained.
In all the houses, those awake
Not for him do wait.
In all the houses now asleep
No one sees him in dreams.
In so many houses he's a stranger
No one knows who he is.

In the big, big city
He has but one and only gate,
And it is locked like all the rest.
And if it doesn't open,
Where will he go in the night?
It is so long till daylight.
Outdoors carouse the whirlwind and the snow,
In every corner drunks and whores.

He knocks on the gate like someone
Who's calling for help in a fire
Light turns on, the sentry opens,
He's been recognized!
Will he let himself be bribed for twenty pennies?
Will he not change his mind?
He is waiting on the stairs
Until the light's extinguished.

And as the light goes out
His fear is melting and he hears:
How rolls down, from step to step
Away from him
The fear…

Each night Israel Aszendorf
Goes home and is afraid
That he may find that
The only gate in town he has,
Will not open again.

From **Miniatures**

On Board Ship

Night. In the bar on board ship the orchestra plays.
The saxophone moans, cries and yawls.
Fizzes the blood in the veins of the dancing pairs.
The movements go faster, wilder, untamed.

It isn't a dance it's a storm.

The people storm but the sea is at rest,
On deck there's a child.
In the third class all are asleep, but
He is awake. He takes out a flute and he plays.
The sea now begins: rocking, one wave leads,
The other holds on,

It isn't a storm, it's a dance.

The ship is listing, almost keeling over.
The dancing pairs, can no longer stand.
They are pale, run to their rooms.
The sea is dancing, but the people lie still,
As if in trance.

The Bird From the Tree I Imagined

Slowly falls the night.
I am leaning on the tree that I imagined.
On the tree that I imagined a bird is singing,
How lovely she sings on the tree that I imagined.
But suddenly the bird cries:
— On the tree that you imagined, I can only sing,
But not build a nest.

Evening

The evening merged with the cow:
The red spots on her skin —
Were taken by the day as it left.
The black spots on her skin —
Were taken by the night as it came.
Even the green grass that she ate —
Flowed from her udders with white moon rays.

Mutes

In the markets they cursed and defamed the lamb —
In speeches and newspapers.
Now, two people are standing at the street corner
Conversing with each other, without a word.
The fish of the land are mute.
Their tongues are in their hands:
Fly in them, pondering magic,
Play on an invisible piano
Weave a bond of mutual friendship.

And if it Happened

And if it happened my love, that you'd be walking in the garden, and the flowers take you prisoner and you will stay with them — then from time to time, when I'd be missing you, I will come close to you, and smell your sweet breath.

And if it happened, my love, that you'd go bathe in the river, and it will not let you out — then from time to time, when I'd be missing you — I'd go into the river and it will seem to me that not the waves, but you are engulfing me.

But if it happened, my love, that you'd be walking in the street on a stormy day, and the wind will pick you up and carry you to heaven, and there you will remain, like a star among the others, then wretched will be my fate! For if I missed you — I would have to wait until the evening.

And until the evening, I will die of longing.

Light

At dawn I lie awake with open eyes
To see how light will fight the dark.
But meanwhile, darkness is a clump of yarn
So great and black.
But into it, the light entwines its threads
The white and black combine.
The white increases more and more,
The black becomes more scarce.
The battle goes on stubbornly,
Bitterly for every object, every step.
A battle for the table: a prisoner of the dark.
The light unties the black threads from its feet — it's free.
A battle for the book-case: light weaves its threads
Struggles for each one and wins. The books
Are conquered by the light.
A landscape on the wall:
Light conquers the first trees, and paints them green.
It paints the sky in blue, it crossed the river with no bridge.
And in the room, light spins its threads around me.
I'm in the light! I'm in the light!
And even though I know that light wins always over dark,
I witness every morning, this struggle from the start:
Like Adam in his first awakening, with fear and doubt.

51722539R00119

Made in the USA
Middletown, DE
04 July 2019